KONTUM DIARY

Kontum DIARY

Captured Writings Bring Peace to a Vietnam Veteran

PAUL REED
and
TED SCHWARZ

THE SUMMIT PUBLISHING GROUP • ARLINGTON, TEXAS

THE SUMMIT PUBLISHING GROUP
One Arlington Centre
1112 East Copeland Road, Fifth Floor
Arlington, Texas 76011

Kontum Diary: Captured Writings Bring Peace to a Vietnam
Veteran

Printed in the United States of America.
00 99 98 97 96   010   5 4 3 2

Library of Congress Cataloging-in-Publication Data

Reed, Paul
    Kontum diary : captured writings bring peace to a Vietnam
veteran / by Paul Reed and Ted Schwarz.
    p. cm.
    ISBN 1-56530-205-2 (hardcover : alk. paper)
    1. Reed, Paul. 2. Nguyên, Văn Nghĩa.
3. Vietnamese Conflict, 1961-1985—Veterans. 4. Vietnamese
Conflict, 1961-1975—Biography. 5. Vietnam—Description and
travel. 6. Veterans—United States—Biography. 7. Veterans—
Vietnam—Biography. I. Schwarz, Ted, 1945- . II Title.
DS559.72R44 1996
959.704'38—dc20   96-5941
                                                      CIP

Cover and book design by David Sims

Dedicated to

NGUYEN VAN NGHIA

for helping me to break free.

CONTENTS

HE HAS BEEN CALLED MANY THINGS, the infantry soldier who takes his rifle, his back pack, and his courage, traveling far from home into a world gone mad with violence. His nickname might be "G.I. Joe," or "Grunt," "Cannon Fodder" or "Unsung Hero." He may endure rain and mud, snow and ice, overwhelming heat or numbing cold. He may walk across a desert or climb endless mountains. And always he faces sudden death from a sniper, a battlefield encounter, or a booby trap along the road. He has left loved ones—parents, a spouse or lover, perhaps children. He has reluctantly, but bravely, abandoned all that is well-known, comforting, and secure in order to fight and perhaps be crippled, maimed for life, or killed thousands of miles from all that is familiar so that the horrors of war might be avoided by those he left behind.

The infantryman is a moralist, filled with a sense of righteousness. He is fighting for a way of life he believes is superior to that of the enemy. He is fighting for a better world as he understands it. He is fighting for all that is good, right, and true. And he is found on both sides of every conflict.

The nobility of the fighting man knows no geographical boundaries. Throughout history, we tell the story of war through the eyes of the victors. Those who win are held to be heroic. Those who lose are considered villains of limited humanity. Yet the soldiers for both sides are always good men, honorable men, each a mirror of the other. Their strengths and weaknesses, their triumphs and failings, are as alike as brothers. Only their language, their race, their politics, or religion are different.

Paul Reed and Nguyen van Nghia were mortal enemies during the Vietnam War. Each held the other in disdain. Each felt that he was fighting for a righteous cause. Each was a hero who condemned the nameless, faceless adversary who was actually himself in a different body, a different land. They might have been the British and the colonials, soldiers for the Union and the Confederacy, or the French and Germans.

Many soldiers never come to understand this reality. They allow their hate and prejudices to fester throughout their lives, never seeing who they are and why they must each come to respect the other when flowers again bloom in the killing fields of their past.

For Paul Reed and Nguyen van Nghia, a diary of thoughts and poetry bridged the hatred of war. In their remarkable story, they learned the lesson some soldiers come to understand only after too many wars, too many tears, and too much needless pain. I am pleased that Paul and dedicated young Americans like him have served under my command, but I regret that their suffering and sacrifices have never been fully acknowledged. My goal since the end of the war has been to correct this. I'm proud of the Vietnam veterans. They served their country well.

Kontum Diary, which recounts the war and its aftermath as experienced by one of those soldiers serves as a classic example. It should offer hope to some and serve as a reminder to others of the respect which is due them.

In closing, I'm thankful that Paul and men like him have experienced the changes described in this book, for by doing such they have become real American heroes.

WILLIAM C. WESTMORELAND
General, United States Army, Retired

P R O L O G U E

by Gerald L. Coffee
Captain, USN retired

THE PROS AND CONS OF THE VIETNAM WAR—the right of the people of South Vietnam to choose against communism, the "domino theory" vis-à-vis the preservation of a non-communist Southeast Asia, the cold and sometimes hot war against monolithic world communism—will be debated by historians for as long as any of us will be alive.

But the story of the Kontum diary, of Paul Reed and Nguyen van Nghia—the story "between the lines"—is not debatable. It is as basic and unequivocal as the sun and the moon.

For Paul Reed, the Kontum diary ripped open old wounds so they could begin to heal properly. His ultimate reunion with his "enemy" hastened the healing even more.

For Nguyen van Nghia, the Kontum diary—finally returned to his possession—enabled him to prove to his wife that he had not only been faithful to her for five long years, but that his memories and thoughts of her had sustained him through his darkest hours.

And for me, a prisoner of war in the communist prisons of Hanoi for over seven years, *Kontum Diary* provided an inspiring reinforcement of my own conclusion: We are all basically the same regardless of the color of our skin, the shape of our eyes, or the sounds of our words. We all laugh and cry, hunger and thirst the same. What separates us? Ideologies! This becomes even clearer when one has seven years just to think about such matters. That is why I was able to come away from my experience without hatred or feelings of vindictiveness toward my captors. The torture and brutality which characterized much of my incarceration were due to the system more than to those individuals who kept me.

Kontum Diary is a poignant confirmation of the ageless and universal dynamic of warriors on opposite sides of the field, of every fighting man's dark, disquieting suspicion that the "other guy" could be a lot like him.

One wonders how much we could accelerate our evolution toward a more civilized planet if our future world leaders could only be privy to each other's diaries before making decisions on war and peace.

Thank you, Paul Reed and Nguyen van Nghia, for sharing your treasure with us.

PREFACE

MY SPECIAL GRATITUDE goes to Jill R. Ewing, for a friendship "above and beyond" the call of duty and from whom the initial idea for this book came—thank you, Jill. Also, this book could not have been completed without the combined efforts of coproducers Steven M. Smith and Philip L. Sturholm of Echo Productions, Seattle, Washington. I'm sincerely thankful for their exhaustive research in locating Mr. Nghia, my trip back to Vietnam to meet him, and their accomplishment in finishing the documentary film titled *Kontum Diary*.

However, neither book nor documentary was possible without the initial endeavor of Mr. Paul Scoles—former Silver Star recipient from C Company, First Battalion, 503rd Infantry Regiment, 173rd Airborne Brigade, paratrooper, and owner of Ironwood Studio in Seattle, Washington. Thank you, Paul, for introducing me to Steve. General William C. Westmoreland deserves my sincere thanks for his time spent in writing his foreword. I am also deeply indebted to Ted Schwarz, my coauthor, for his discernment of my feelings, his hard work, and also his dedication to the principles I wanted the book to promote. At Summit Publishing Group, Arlington, Texas, I'm grateful for Len Oszustowicz, Dee Richardson, David Sims, Brent Lockhart, and the remaining staff, including those two hard-working editors, Mark Murphy and Bill Scott. I'd like to thank my son, Silas, for bearing with me through the hard times and also for his support. My parents, Polly and Leo L. Baker, are to be commended for honoring my March 17, 1968, request of them to safeguard Mr. Nghia's property. I'm very thankful they did! For support, encouragement, and safekeeping of Mr. Nghia's NLF flag for better than twenty-five years, Jim Davis (also known as "Diamond

Jim Davis"), the former commanding officer of A/1/503rd Infantry, 173rd Airborne Brigade, earns my appreciation. For giving their account of what happened during the battle of Hill 1064, their support, encouragement, and friendship, I thank Lewis "Stoney" Stoneking (B/1/503rd), David Harman (A/1/503rd), Bill "Billy Joe" Jang (D/1/503rd), John B. Doane (former November platoon leader A/1/503rd), and Richard "Goon" Ortler (A/1/503rd)—all former 173rd Airborne Brigade personnel. Thank you, Dale Doucet, for helping me to see the importance of returning Mr. Nghia's diary. Being there and encouraging me when I needed it most were my friends at the Dallas Vet Center, David Rodriguez, Dr. Matt Menger, Mrs. Cross, Ed Brown, and Sandy Johnson. To Vic Royal (former A Company, 173rd Airborne buddy wounded and evacuated from Kontum—now deceased because of cancer), thank you for all your inspiration. May you rest in peace, brother.

A very special thanks goes to the following people, companies, and organizations: The U.S. Army & Joint Services Environment Group, Washington, DC for research; Nguyen Vinh, coworker and friend of Jill Ewing and first translator of the diary; Rose and Jim Baldree for support; Vincent Nguyet, second translator of the diary; Captain Gerald Coffee, former POW, motivational speaker, and author of *Beyond Survival* for, of course, motivation; Rick Murphy, the third and final translator of the diary; James Sargent for help in locating Jim Davis; David Hale Smith and Shelley Lewis of DHS Literary for continued support and for successfully representing this book; Independent Television Service, Inc., of St. Paul, Minnesota, for grant money and making possible the production of the film, *Kontum Diary*. Thanks to all their staff, especially to their stations relations manager, Gayle Loeber, publicity manager, Nancy Robinson, and outreach coordinator, Suzanne Stenson; The Rockefeller Foundation for their financial gift toward production of *Kontum Diary*; William "Bill" Thornton; Gary Gullickson, compiler and coauthor of *Viet Nam: Our Story, One On One,* for inspiring me to write this book; Steve Blow, writer for *The Dallas Morning News*; Ruben C. "Sugar Bear" Johnson of the Texas Association of Vietnam Veterans for all the pain and sacrifice he's had to endure which inspired me; Jim Douglas of

Channel 5 News in Fort Worth, Texas for being a sensitive person and for caring; J.W. "Doc" Fudge of the Dallas Veterans Administration office for care, support, and understanding; Steve Maus; Al "Big Al" Fuchs for prayerful support; Edith and Wes Drawbaugh for our special friendship; Mike Spradlin and the congregation of First Covenant Church of Irving, Texas, for prayerful support and concern; Marc C. Waszkiewicz; Mike James; Bob and Nancy Jamieson for being extremely supportive and for buying all those lunches for the hungry, broke writer; Ron Long, owner of Custom Video Services of Addison, Texas, (and his partner Mark Lazarow) for their thoughtful dedication and support; Dang Minh Nguyet, foreign relations specialist with the People's Committee of Thai Binh Province, Vietnam, for noteworthy assistance in communication with Mr. Nghia; The Ministry of Foreign Affairs, Hanoi, Vietnam, for cooperation and assistance in locating Mr. Nguyen van Nghia and family; Do Cong Minh, Director, Foreign Press Service, Ministry of Foreign Affairs, Hanoi, Vietnam; Luong Thanh Nghi, translator and press officer of the Ministry of Foreign Affairs, Hanoi, Vietnam; Nguyen van Luong, driver and press officer of the Ministry of Foreign Affairs, Hanoi, Vietnam; Pham Quang Khanh; Bui Manh Hung; John K. Cook, marine Vietnam combat veteran and former Texas Veterans Commission veterans service officer, for continuous support, understanding, and friendship; the Society of the 173rd Airborne Brigade (Separate), specifically the men of Chapter XIII, the Texas chapter, for constant comradeship and backing; Sam Boyd; Donald H. Souder for translations; John Nguyen-the-Suc for translation work. For writing the poetry in that small book, I'd especially like to thank Mr. Nguyen van Nghia.

Finally, and perhaps most important, I'd like to thank God, who, being sovereign over all things, initiated this work a long time ago, and who, by using a simple thing like a small diary, changed my heart.

PAUL REED

Paul Reed and Nguyen van Nghia, November 1993

CHAPTER ONE

L et all sort of warlike operations, whether they befall you now in your own time, or hereafter in the times of your posterity, be done out of your own borders: but when you are about to go to war, send ambassages and heralds to those who are your voluntary enemies, for it is a right thing to make use of words to them before you come to your weapons of war; and assure them thereby, that although you have a numerous army, with horses and weapons, and, above these, a God merciful to you, and ready to assist you, you do however desire them not to compel you to fight against them, nor to take from them what they have, which will be our gain, but what they will have no reason to wish we should take to ourselves...

Lead an army pure, and of chosen men, composed of all such as have extraordinary strength of body and hardiness of soul; but do you send away the timorous part, lest they run away in the time of action, and so afford an advantage to your enemies.

Flavius Josephus, *circa AD 30*

Had it not been for the army, the two men would probably never have met. Compulsory military service was the great leveler of the 1960s for those who did not use education as a means of avoiding the draft. Rich and poor, college educated and high school dropouts, sophisticates and small-town boys, they all were equal in the eyes of the generals.

Certainly, this was the case with the two men—one who became an officer in the army, the other a "grunt" infantryman paratrooper. The latter was a Southerner, a youth whose life was good times, wild adventures, and chasing girls. He was highly intelligent, and his parents hoped he would go on to college and enter a profession. But he was too restless for that and saw no reason to push himself. His interests were fast cars, fast motorcycles, and fast girls. That was why he would do anything for a dare or a laugh, including riding a motorcycle through the halls of Hillcrest High School in Dallas, Texas. His friends thought he was "cool." His principal didn't.

The other man was almost a generation older, a Northerner, interested in art, politics, and poetry. Had they met anywhere outside the military, he would have been contemptuous of the stereotypical "good old boy" from the South.

Not that the older man had been without his share of youthful wildness. His rucksack still held pictures of attractive young women he had met when moving from town to town, village to village, as his unit traveled the enemy's land. Some of the women who pressed their photographs into his hand were enamored with men in uniform, no matter for which side they fought. Others were politically sympathetic, the picture a reminder of secret support in the midst of those whose smiles, waves, and seemingly friendly gestures masked hatred and a desire to drive the soldiers from their land.

The older soldier politely thanked some of the women who gave him their pictures, and flirted with others. He knew that the gesture was part of the local culture in the alien land through which he traveled. But he also knew that there was a simmering sensuality lurking behind the gesture in just enough instances that had he wanted to cheat on his wife, there would have been no difficulty in finding an attractive, willing partner. Yet casual sex was not his desire, and though he retained all the photographs, his thoughts were focused on the woman he left behind.

The younger man, like so many new recruits, was still a captive of his raging hormones. Only the older man understood the fulfillment of marriage, of family, of the inner peace and intense joy that comes from monogamy. He had no need to prove his manhood other than finding a way to stay alive in the killing fields until his tour of duty was over. He sought no adventure, as the younger man would do. He had long ago come to understand that after the first battle, everyone's focus is on home, loved ones, and the stability they all left behind.

My life is the army;
You are married to a soldier.
Lying here I miss you,
Aching throughout this winter night.
I cannot contain my desire to come home
As my annual ten-day leave draws near.
Sighing I count the days,
Pining for each next one to come.
The colder the wind, the more I miss you.
Lying here this winter night, who can I tell all this to?
Midwatch, morning watch...

Sleepless nights pass, each watch grows longer.
Thoughts of seeing you still consume me.
Who can stand this war, this kind of life
I find myself lamenting to the moon.
The more I think about you, the greater my sorrow.
We have missed out on so much.
Friends our age have raised families by now.
I envy them so, husband and wife working side by side
     each day.
They go to sleep, then awaken to the sight of each other.
They are like pairs of white doves.
While we each go our own lonely way.

I dream the resistance has won peace.
I lie next to you, whispering your name.
But you don't answer me in my deep sleep.
Suddenly the rooster crows in morning watch;
We are both alone again.
My head clears, I again painfully realize
It will be many months before I see you again.
I resign myself to endure to the end,
Until the country is reunified.
So I can come home.

The older man wrote this poem down in a little book that he carried in his rucksack. He considered putting the words in a letter to his wife, but that might be too painful. He knew his own heart was true, but in his loneliness, there were too many fears (needless fears, he later learned) about his vibrant, attractive wife, alone and unfulfilled so many miles away. He longed for her to understand what he was enduring, yet he also knew she could never fully comprehend the fear, the anger, and the constant sense of loss as yet another friend was felled. Rather than risk more pain, he comforted himself with a second poem, written as though his wife had sent it to him.

> My love, you joined the army to serve your country.
> Troubled, I yet advised you to go defend your native land.
> We embrace, oh my dear
> Never embrace another.
> Please always remember the flute you gave me.
> Remember our promises to remain forever faithful.
> Though far apart, I will always be waiting for you
> I stand here in the rice fields at day's end;
> Mist clouds the horizon.
>
> My little flute melody
> Has been carried off by the wind.
> It is for the one I love
> Miles and miles away.
> The rice shouts with glee in the fields
> The blooming flowers renew my hope.
> I sew this shirt with my love
> To send to my faraway soldier.
> Though far apart
> I will always be waiting for you
> I am always with you.

Paul Reed was too naive to know such sentiments. While the older man had experienced military service in an earlier war, Paul knew about combat only from television, motion pictures, and the fantasies he had woven over the years. His father, a petroleum engineer, had been a first lieutenant in an army ordnance division in

World War II. He never talked about the adventures his son was certain he had experienced. But Paul played with the uniform, insignias, medals, and equipment belt his father had kept as souvenirs and imagined himself in the same adventures. Paul's childhood play included imaginary travels to Europe where he heroically triumphed over the Nazis in terrible hand-to-hand combat. Because he never asked, he didn't realize that his father's medical condition had prevented him from serving overseas and so he had spent his entire tour of duty stateside.

Craving the adventure of jumping out of planes, Paul decided to enlist in the U.S. Army in October 1966. He made this decision privately, telling neither his parents nor the girl he had been dating. He had always been something of a loner and (like the paratroopers) fancied himself set apart from the norm. He certainly had no interest in higher education. At any rate, he was less than attractive to college recruiters because of all the trouble he'd gotten into in high school. In the most recent incident, he cut one of his classes just before the final exams at the end of his senior year. The principal, determined to teach him a lesson, suspended him for three days. This meant that he would not be able to take the exams and thus would not graduate.

Paul's mother did not approve of his behavior, but she did not want to see him suspended. She marched to the principal's office, demanding that Paul be allowed to take the tests. When the principal resisted, she reminded him that such a failure could not be made up in summer school. Instead, Paul would be required by state law to repeat his senior year. Horrified by this thought, the principal agreed that the suspension would not be enforced.

When Paul walked into the army recruiting office, his only thoughts were of how much fun it would be to jump out of planes and float back to earth. The army would be an adventure, like Boy Scouts or the outings of the Methodist youth group at his church. There would be guns and violence, but they weren't a concern. He was only five feet and ten inches tall and so skinny that he looked like a tent pole. The idea that he would get paid to jump out of planes overshadowed any other thinking.

The recruiting office was sparsely finished, the primary decorations being posters urging the youths who entered to "be all that you can be" in today's army. The steel desks were heavy, seemingly built to the same specifications as military tanks. The floor was linoleum, the chairs made of hardwood. The only accommodation to comfort in the entire office was the armrests on these chairs.

The recruiter, Staff Sergeant (E-6) Russell, fit Paul's image of what a paratrooper should be. Well over six feet tall, lean, hard, and broad shouldered, he looked the well-trained professional in his regulation crew cut and khaki uniform. He also knew the right things to say to convince Paul to join.

Army airborne, the service Paul wanted, was a special life for the few who could be a part of it. Most could not succeed. The training was rigorous, too tough for many boys Paul's age. But Sgt. Russell would look carefully at Paul, as though sizing him up, then say that he thought Paul might have what it took to succeed. The combination of subtle challenge and reinforcement of Paul's fantasies was just the right touch needed to get a new enlistee. Paul signed the paperwork without leaving the office to think about what he would be doing for the next three years of his life. He agreed to take twenty-four hours to get packed, then would ship out the next day following the successful completion of his physical exam, a formality.

As soon as the paperwork was completed, Paul was shown a private area so that he could call his mother. The excitement in his voice should have been infectious, or so he believed. He knew how much trouble he had been for his parents during the past couple of years. He had graduated only because his mother convinced the principal to let him take his exams. But he had already planned to join the army a year ago and had completed his senior year only because his father had convinced him that nothing in life would come easily without a diploma.

By signing the enlistment papers, he had done something honorable. He was going to be army airborne, jumping out of planes, serving his country, being the first line of defense against anyone who would dare take on the most powerful nation in the world. How proud they would be of their son! How thrilled that their ne'er-do-well was about to have heroic adventures! All the weeping, all the recriminations would be wiped away by the action he had taken. That was why he was so surprised to hear his mother burst into tears.

Paul Reed had never talked with his parents about Vietnam. He had heard of the land and knew of the fighting because he had seen stories about what was happening on television for the past year. But no one he knew was affected by the Southeast Asian nation so many thousands of miles away. His next-door neighbor, Brendan, a boy about the age of his sister, had served with the army airborne in Germany, having a wonderful time, getting into great shape, and returning home unscathed. His church choir director's son was also in the army, and Paul assumed that the youth's experiences were like Brendan's. (He did not know that the boy was being sent to Vietnam and would be killed in action before Paul even got there.) He understood adventure, not the realities of a culture in turmoil and the ramifications of Americans being sent to support one of the sides.

His mother knew, though. She knew that the military was not the Boy Scouts. She recognized that a boy with no academic background and nothing to offer the army other than the ability to fight and die would have the least chance for survival if the war became more intense. That was why she had fought so hard for him to be able to graduate. That was why she wept when he told her he had made what they both knew was an irreversible decision about his future.

Little was said during Paul's last night at home. He was eighteen, legally a man, though still so young that his body would not reach its full height of six feet until after his tour of duty. His mother held him, cried, and could not give him the emotional support he hoped to receive. His father said nothing at all, showed no emotion; it was just another night at home, another family dinner, another quiet evening despite the intense emotions of his wife.

This was partly because Paul and his father were never close, though each respected the other. Paul thought he was being just like his dad when he enlisted, not knowing that his father's World War II adventures were all in the boy's imagination. In fact, his father was proud that his son had finally taken a positive step in life, even if it was not the one he would have preferred. Yet to show any sort of support would mean further upsetting his wife.

Ultimately, the family members spent the night with their differing thoughts. The next day, Paul's father went to work and his mother drove Paul downtown to get his physical. He passed easily, then boarded the bus that carried him to basic training.

I miss my mother, her warm smile,
In the kitchen tending a fiery stove
On a starry night.
I recall the painful separation
Of a mother from her young son.
For not even a second have I abandoned my post.
I am here for my parents, braving the wind,
A proud soldier of this bridge, of my people.

> — *A poem by one of his friends which Second Lieutenant Nguyen van Nghia kept in his book of memories.*

CHAPTER TWO

The book was small, meant to be carried in the pocket so that it would always be at hand. It was the mark of a man with some education, though how the owner used it revealed much about his character. Some made terse notes about where they had been each day, treating it a little like a desk calendar. Others used it to record ideas they read or information they heard that they thought would be of value to them.

For a few, such as Second Lieutenant Nguyen van Nghia, the book served a higher purpose. It was the repository of thoughts and feelings too important to risk forgetting. He titled it "Memories" and carefully recorded on its pages the love, hate, loneliness, fear, physical hardship, isolation from family, and the loneliness of a soldier immersed in violent combat far from home.

He would often read aloud from it to his comrades, who took comfort from it. Some words in the book could only have been uttered in such poetry. Only in this way could he express the feelings for his wife that would normally be restricted to the privacy of the bedroom. But their separation had lasted years, and by writing in the book, he could fantasize that he was telling the woman he loved what was in his heart. It was also only in these poems that he could admit to the fear and loneliness that were a soldier's constant companions. The book was his unique diary—not a day-by-day account of activities, but a window to his soul and to that of his friends. For others who read it later, it was witness to the indomitable strength of the human spirit.

A Lullaby

Days then months pass
A year is twelve months, each with thirty days.
You sit, numbering the days.
Fully six years have passed since I left.
That day your rosy cheeks were flush with youth.
Their brightness still warms me.

The good old days lapsed into
Ongoing struggle.
At home you still try to stay busy
Autumn leaves have fallen six times since I left.
You lean against the door, facing the river hoping.
You lift your gaze to the rosy clouds overhead.
You look 'round the yard hoping
But still see nothing.

The day I left I promised
That I would return.
I will keep my promise.
You've lost yourself in tending the rice fields
Since the day I left 'til now.
At home you are still daily hoping;
Your love is like pink silk.
How can I write all that I think of you?

You are a bird, feathered in lotus petals.
What could be brighter than the glow of us together?
The greatest love is yours.
As I lean against this light pole during midwatch,
I gaze at your picture and return your smile;
So sweet is your expression.
Our love is like the sunrise
Shedding light through rosy clouds.
Missing me you think up some verse
With this pen I will jot it down.

I am awkward; I don't know what to say.
How will I finish this letter
My heart is bursting.

Though far apart
The distance does not separate us.
We remain joined
In the spring of our lives.

The national history and culture of Vietnam are no less complex
and opaque than the poetry of Lieutenant Nghia's diary. They go
far back into legendary times of dragons and fairy princesses—
the first known dynasty in the area is believed to have been
established nearly five thousand years ago, although most schol-
ars would say that the ethnic term "Vietnamese" applies only to
the last twenty-three hundred years or so. These people, known
as the "Viet" tribe, lived in what is now the northern part of
Vietnam. They were in the Chinese sphere of influence, and
from the Chinese view, were the southernmost part of China. In
fact, the ancient meaning of "Viet" is "south." (Interestingly, the
modern meaning of "nam" is also "south.") Unlike others in the
Chinese sphere, though, the Vietnamese successfully resisted
assimilation into Chinese culture and society.

Indeed, resistance to domination by outsiders is a funda-
mental part of Vietnamese culture. Rebellions have always
risen on a fairly regular basis. One of the most famous occurred
in AD 39 and produced the first military heroines in the country's history.

Sisters Trung Trach and Trung Nhi were born to wealth and
privilege and could have lived comfortably under Chinese domination. Nevertheless, Trung Trach became the leader of a rebellion. After gathering a secret army, she and her sister went to
the Hung Mountain shrine to pray. They then led their followers
into battles that ultimately proved successful against the occupying force. The Chinese were compelled to withdraw, and in AD
40, Trung Trach was declared the nation's queen. She ruled for
four years before the Chinese returned with enough fighting
strength to recapture the land. The sisters are said to have committed suicide rather than suffer in defeat.

The story of the sisters became a part of history, folklore,
and song, as did the leaders of subsequent revolts. But it was the
memory of the sisters that created a degree of cultural confusion
for the Vietnamese. These were people who looked upon men as
superior. The man was supposed to care for the family, earn the

living, and run his home a little like a benign dictatorship. Yet whenever there was prolonged war, the women would abandon the roles expected of them and do whatever was necessary to preserve their homes. Sometimes this meant taking a more active role in the fields where they were raising crops. At other times it meant taking up weapons and acting as assassins, guerrilla fighters, and members of an unpredictable resistance that could be deceptively innocent until the women struck.

There was another change caused by the periodic occupations and annexations of land. The original culture kept changing in the occupied territories, the citizens adapting by mixing faiths and philosophical ideas. Buddhism, Confucianism, Catholicism, and other concepts blended into the culture.

Astrology has also been important to the Vietnamese, as is the acceptance of suffering in order to attain a better next life. The latter was a major factor in the willingness of the people to endure all manner of hardships in any war they felt was important to the future of the country. This was also a major area of misunderstanding for the enemies of the Vietnamese who, one by one over the centuries, always lost control of the land they had conquered. Sometimes the escape from occupation took a brief period of time. Sometimes it took several lifetimes. But there could never be too much suffering, because the people believed that such continuous trauma would ultimately help them lead a better next life.

The last major Asian intervention in Vietnam came with another Chinese conquest of the land in 1406. Twelve years later, a leader named Le Loi began a guerrilla war against the Chinese occupiers. He and his followers endured for ten years, conquering their enemy and restoring an independent nation in 1428. This freedom from outside domination would last for 360 years and permitted an expansion into the area recently known as South Vietnam, where settlers displaced the native population.

For nearly four centuries, Vietnam was governed sometimes by regional leaders and sometimes by rulers from either the North or South who managed to unify the country by force. During this period, significant differences developed between the people of the South and the people of the North, but they all thought of themselves as part of the same cultural identity, as Vietnamese. There were three important institutions in their lives—family, village, and state. Thus, no matter what the political realities of the moment, most people always felt that just as the family and the village have one leader, so the country should be united under one leader.

In the nineteenth century, the West became heavily involved in Vietnam. The French army captured Da Nang in 1858. With that colony firmly established, the French successively went after Saigon, the Delta region, and, in 1883, all of the North. France effectively gained full control of the country that became known as French Indochina.

French domination radically changed the Vietnamese culture. By the time Nguyen van Nghia was born, the Chinese model of government had almost entirely disappeared from every city, town, and village. Instead, there were managers and administrators of a type identical to what could be routinely found in the West. By the time the United States got involved in the military action, Vietnam was one of the most literate nations on the planet.

The Catholic Church gained prestige. Old values were questioned. Modern technology altered the ways people earned a living and interacted with each other. The old Imperial Courts were allowed to continue, and hereditary titles remained. But such leaders had no influence. They were figureheads enjoying the perquisites of power without the authority. Despite that, they retained a place in the culture much like European monarchs who had become figureheads. The last person to bear the title "emperor" did not leave power until 1945.

Most important of all were differences in the way France governed the North and the South. Traditional institutions of authority were pretty much left intact in the North, and the French governed through them. But in the South, direct rule significantly weakened the power of the village and altered the nature of the social and political structures, without providing viable alternatives.

The Vietnamese fought for France during World War II, but when it was over, as Europe was trying to recover from the radical changes brought by the conflict, the Viet Minh began a campaign to take back the country. Soon Hanoi, Hue, and even Saigon returned to Vietnamese control. This rebellion was spearheaded by Northerners who, like the Chinese, had moved from Confucianism to communism, and was most effective in the North. Conditions in the South were so chaotic that the Viet Minh had little more success than anyone else in organizing the region. Thus, they were content in the armistice agreement of 1954 to have a boundary line drawn between North and South. But they never saw this as the creation of a permanent sovereign state, just as one more temporary period in history when Vietnam would not be unified under one leader.

Nguyen van Nghia's education was an unusual one. Although the French still dominated the land, a number of old and new ideas had come together to build an internal resistance that was capable of overthrowing the occupying government. Part of this was Western in nature, including knowledge gained by studying the French Revolution as well as the social, economic, and political theories of Marx and Engels. And part of this was ancient, the idea of life always being in balance.

The Vietnamese peasants had long believed that balance and order were the natural states of existence. If you were to be in good health, there had to be a proper mix of different foods as well as a proper maintenance of relationships within the family and the community. In addition, proper behavior, learned from schoolteachers and from interacting with adults in the greater society, was understood to help assure happiness and prosperity.

A country under foreign domination is not in balance. Many of the people saw that the health of their nation and the prosperity of their families depended on restoring Vietnam to self-rule.

By 1954, when the French had been ousted from Vietnam and the country was divided into two parts, the Republic of South Vietnam was a nation with significant problems in its traditional social institutions. The people had been in the midst of violence during the fight against the French, which had lasted approximately twenty years. They were tired of war, and though they would continue fighting, their hearts were not in the effort. There also was limited moral leadership. The old authorities had weakened to impotence, but there was no universally accepted replacement. Although most people lived lives of traditional virtue, the interaction with Western society had created a new, less desirable element. Those involved in prostitution, black marketeering, gambling, and extortion rackets came to have significant influence in the business and culture of the larger cities. The country was also dependent on outside economies— one reason why the people were so anxious for American support. Many of the people needed economic support as much as the govenment needed political and military support.

By contrast, the Communist leaders of the North, though not without problems, were able to effectively inspire the people to common action. With traditional institutions of power still functioning, they were able to expand the old virtues of loyalty to family and village to include loyalty to the Party and its leader, Ho Chi Minh ("the one who enlightens").

Neither government could be called humanitarian, and both were notorious for human rights violations, both of their own citizens and of prisoners captured in battle.

An irreconcilable difference in viewpoint developed between the leaders of the North and the supporters of the South. The Southern allies viewed North Vietnamese-supported resistance as aggression by a foreign power. They never understood the nationalism of the North, but saw Vietnam as part of a global Communist threat in terms of what came to be called the domino theory: If one Southeast Asian nation became Communist, all of them would, one after the other, just like a row of dominoes toppling over. The North Vietnamese, however, saw themselves as acting in traditional ways—resisting foreign occupation, restoring balance, and reuniting the nation.

There were other differences as well. The Northerners were viewed as intellectuals of limited practical skills by the Southerners. They were mocked for their sophistication since it did not seem to serve a useful purpose.

By contrast, the Northerners saw the Southerners as uncouth, lacking purpose, moral fiber, and a direction that would benefit the people. The hostility was very much like what occurred in the United States between the Northern New England intellectuals of Harvard, Yale, Vassar, Smith, and other elite colleges and universities, and the "good old boy" image of some less well-educated, unpolished Southerners.

Despite all this, the feelings of most soldiers called to go to war in the South following the liberation of the country from French domination were ones of sadness. They had little interest in what was taking place, except in the case of those who saw

the military action as an adventure. They believed in the unification of the country, of the restoring of balance to everyone's
lives, but this was still an alien land. They could as much relate
to the people of the South as North Americans can relate to the
cultures of Mexico, Chile, or Colombia.

> I stand here watching the enemy
> Forcing civilians to build bunkers.
> Many the age of my mother and father labor at gunpoint.
> Infants cry out to be breast-fed,
> But the mothers must work.
> Often I seethe with rage,
> Chafing before the division of this nation.
>
> Month after month I meet enemy soldiers
> So how can I avoid sorrow?
> We are of one blood, one race.
> Brother, how can you be such a traitor!
> The road you are on is full of blood and sin.

> *— Nguyen van Nghia, writing about having to
> watch the South Vietnamese as they kept
> their citizens working on the war effort
> against the people of the North.*

The North Vietnamese Army (NVA) did not have the wealth of
the U.S. Army, but it was far from inadequate for its purpose. It
was experienced, disciplined, and had able leaders, sound tactics, and extremely sophisticated psychological support for the
troops. There were newsletters sent to the men which support-
ed their efforts and trained them for battle when they were great
distances from the North. Typical was one which discussed
"How To Make Our Attack Effective." It read, in part:

> *If we want to attack our enemy and be victorious,
> it requires willingness and planning ahead of the nec-
> essary tactics. We must work well at the enemy's posi-
> tion and use the weather conditions to our advantage.
> It is one of the enemy's weaknesses. So today we want*

to discuss these matters with the troops so they can become masters at this tactic.

The newsletter posed three questions: "How do we attack the enemy in surprise and put them in a panic situation?"; "If the enemy has more men than we do and their unit is bigger than ours, how can we attack and destroy them?"; and "What kind of weapons should we use to destroy our enemy effectively?"

The letter continued:

There are some tactics that only soldiers and Liberation Army can use because these tactics were created and designed in our blood. We have to face him and come close to the enemy without second thought, to surprise him from every direction.

We come in with our courage in our hand and use it as our advanced weapon.

When we get to within 40-100 feet we are in an advanced position. We must then wait for the slowing down of the artillery shelling. We must pinpoint everything. Remember, at this time the enemy will be in defensive posture and we are in offensive posture. All we do is just show up and take over. We are fighting for our home and always in this fighting situation, it doesn't matter what happens.

These exercises are not easy, but they require much more study in order for us to become masters in these fighting tactics. After we become experts, we must keep on trying and learning from our mistakes. Always stay alert and be combat-ready. We must always stay in small groups and keep some distance between us. Attack small groups of enemy and avoid big enemy groups or units.

We get information about the enemy from civilians to support our tactics, which can help our soldiers sneak in at night from everywhere. In the meantime, our artillery shells fall on the enemy targets.

With open minds and observations of our soldiers, we can have success and win the battle. We always approach the enemy in groups of one or two to get their attention in one direction, then the main group attacks from another direction with the support of artillery.

Every group of our soldiers has a special task to attack the enemy. Each group must review and come up with thoughts to adjust the condition of our tactics.

This article combines information on strategy with psychological support: "Today, every single battle we fight we win with high spirit because we are trained well. Our every move seems to work together as gears in a wheel or machine. When our soldiers get close to the enemy, they create confusion and panic. Our soldiers take advantage of moonlight to use our tactics effectively, which includes artillery shelling."

There were also contests to see who could be most successful in battle before national celebrations related to past revolutions. Headlines were supportive of the special celebration of successes on the battlefield, including: "We killed more than four thousand invading Americans"; "We destroyed three battalions and twenty-two companies"; "We shot down 184 jets and destroyed 150 tanks, vehicles and 40 cannons"; and "We burned almost five million liters of their gasoline."

The North Vietnamese were unlike other enemies Americans had fought over the years. They saw the unification of their country as the most important goal for themselves and their children. They were able to keep themselves supplied. And they had a cultural history that encouraged them to endure prolonged effort against seemingly insurmountable odds. Whether or not they could have been beaten does not matter. The people, the countryside, and the attitudes were different from what the Chinese, the French, and the Americans expected.

Below is an excerpt from a letter Paul Reed sent to his parents, trying to explain some of the Vietnamese culture.

May 18, 1968

Mom & Dad,

You wanted to know a little about the Montagnards, well it was kind of hard talking to this man as the S. Viets can hardly understand them in their own language. The Montagnards are basically good people, they don't steal and they work hard for their food, whereas most S. Viets expect the U.S. to give them everything. The S. Viets dislike the Montagnards. I don't know why. I suppose its like the Mexicans & Negroes in S. Tex. The Montagnards are a separate class of people and they wear very little clothes, like natives of Africa, they also live in the mountains. Every once in a while a tribe comes in from the mountains and the U.S. puts them in reservations in order to protect them & give them a better place to live. We like to get them out of the mountains so we can artillery & B-52 where they were. They also have dark skin, almost as dark as some dark Negroes. You will find very few S. Viets without Montagnard blood in them. I saw a pure Vietnamese woman the other day, white skinned, she was pretty fair looking. Also saw a good looking girl which isn't often.

Yesterday, I saw a mammasan carrying some firewood to her house, and she was about 100 yds from it so I offered to help her. Boy was that a mistake. She was carrying a good 100 lbs. and she's no bigger than you, Mom, it almost killed me but I made it. I did it to show my appreciation for her sewing up a hole in my pants. One day I was over by her house and some little kids were making fun of my pants so she came out & sewed it up. I guess she heard the little kids.

Word has come over the loudspeaker;
We are to head South
My beloved home village fades in the distance.

I miss the harvest season
I miss the girls of home
Hair longer than one's outstretched arm.
Now the girls valiantly defend our village.
Hue knows peace and tranquillity;
The Perfume River sings.
My native village knows hunger.
Every night the echoes of Southern gunfire
Tear at my insides.

From My Heart of Hearts

The enemy guns thunder
More madly with each passing moment.
Marking the fall of many of my friends;
They will never know life again.
The motherland weeps for them.
How can we possibly surrender?
We are the proud soldiers of the bridge,
Bearers of the Party's teachings.
We must silence the enemy,
Still them like glassy waters.

I stand here, defending factories and farms.
Day and night they bustle with activity
So the motherland will be blessed in wartime.
I stand here so my sister can attend school,
So our village can ever greet the new year.
I stand here at the demarcation line
Looking South; remembering North.
I am divided like the land.

Affection

My rifle firmly in hand
I cannot leave this land.
I love this land of the bridge's end
Where I have stood guard these seven years.
The pines of Vinh Linh tower upward forever,
I love the rows of folksy houses.
The wind unfurls the Star Flag.
Still, I miss the family hearth.
I picture the road of my native village,
A small lantern shining at each home's gate.

My troops by my side
Bring warmth to my soul.
I wish the country was no longer divided
So we could be together as friends...

CHAPTER THREE

Like many recruits, Paul Reed looked upon the basic training he received at Fort Polk, Louisiana, as Boy Scout camp with live ammunition. These young men didn't have a clue that America was at war. They all knew about Vietnam from television news, though it didn't seem too important. American involvement was still limited enough that few of them knew anyone who had been sent to fight. Fewer still had heard of anyone dying there.

Reed was so naive when he enlisted that he took great pride in being informed that he would hold the rank of private (E-1), the very lowest military rank. No one had ever given him a rank before. No one had ever told him he could have a title. At eighteen, this was the most exciting moment of his life, followed closely by the news that he was being assigned the Military Occupational Specialty (MOS) of 11 Bravo (11B). Again, the honor was dubious. An 11 Bravo was infantry, a grunt, the most basic form of soldier with no special technological training. The ancient term "cannon fodder" has always referred to infantry privates. But Paul didn't think about this.

Like his comrades, he took pride in the fact that the ground troops were always the first line of defense in any war. Throughout history, they had been the ones who directly confronted the enemy. They were the ones who determined the success or failure of battlefield encounters. They were the ones with the courage to mop up after a bombing or intense shelling of enemy territory. Paul had hoped for a different option, yet was thrilled with the assignment and delighted to receive ninety-three dollars a month in pay, a figure that would rise to $148 per month when he finished jump school.

Fort Polk was little different from any other army base. Staff Sergeant Jim Beam met the new recruits upon their arrival—just before 10:00 P.M. He was short, no more than five-feet-six-inches tall. He wore the drill instructor's uniform complete with a Smokey the Bear hat that made him look like a cuddly teddy bear. He seemed the kind of man who grew up with some over-ly perfumed, heavily made-up, overweight aunt crushing him to her bosom, pinching his cheeks, and calling him her "cute little man." But he was hard as a rock, growled like a grizzly bear, and was so intimidating that men twice his size would not challenge his authority. "I'm just like the liquor, Jim Beam. You may think I'm smooth for a while, but your head'll find out different later."

The training started immediately—marching and standing in formation until well after midnight. Paul and his fellow recruits were informed that they were no longer sons, brothers, husbands, or lovers. They were soldiers who belonged to Staff Sergeant Beam for the next two months. Whatever he said, they would do.

Exhausted but happy, Reed got a few hours' sleep before having his head shaved, receiving inoculations, and being issued four pairs of olive-drab fatigues. He was a soldier, and he was determined to be the best there was. He desperately wanted approval for his actions, and he was going to make Staff Sergeant Beam—his surrogate parent—proud.

The idea of war was never real during basic training. There was talk of the enemy, but it was always unnamed, like a coach talking about rival teams during the high school football season. Paul was taught a little bit about fighting maneuvers and defen-sive tactics, but these were based on the assumption that war-fare would again take place in the European theater. Confrontations would be on open land masses with large num-bers of troops confronting one another, much like what had occurred in France, Germany, and Italy during World War II. There would be large numbers of soldiers. There would be occa-sional close combat. But there was no talk of jungle warfare, of guerrilla tactics, of becoming involved in a civil war.

In hindsight, Paul Reed realized that he had turned from his family to the army for approval. Nothing about his high school years had been quite right for him. He had shown disrespect towards his teachers and the principal. He had run with the boys and girls who did not see education as important. He wanted his parents to respect his actions, to tell him he was doing a good job as a person, but they didn't, and he knew he did not deserve such praise. He had accomplished nothing that they valued. He barely completed high school, while his sister was nearing the end of her college undergraduate years. Even his job at the supermarket promised no career. It was only part time, a way to earn money to pay for the "toys" of older teenagers. He had no purpose, no direction, and when he finally took the action that he thought would please them, his mother seemed to be personally affronted. The fact that she understood better than he did what might lay ahead for him affected her emotions and denied him the praise he craved.

Basic training was a way of winning approval. The closed society of the army gave Paul Reed a new chance for success, for respect, to be told he was doing something worthwhile, not just thinking only of the moment's pleasure. And when he was finished, he was one of only 10 percent of his class recommended for immediate promotion to private first class (PFC).

It was in advanced infantry training (AIT) that the Boy Scout Camp image faded from Reed's mind. The barracks had originally been built to house German prisoners of war brought to the United States during World War II. They were sparse, with outdoor latrines and coal-burning space heaters for those times when the temperature dropped near freezing. The space heaters filled the room with black smoke that clung to Reed's hair and clothing, irritating his lungs so that he frequently choked. He eventually spent several days in the hospital with a lung problem brought about by breathing the coal smoke.

Sleep was limited. The young men were pushed to their limits, some of them so angry and exhausted that they decided to leave. But Reed kept seeing what he was doing as a way of proving himself. He hated the life he was leading, though if this was what he had to experience in order to succeed, then so be it. He was determined to be the best soldier possible.

AIT involved much more realistic combat training than basic training had. The instructors were focusing on Vietnam, and they had a sense of urgency that came from knowing that many of these new soldiers would actually see combat. The problem of transforming that urgency to the trainees, who were still fairly complacent, was a difficult one to solve. Each instructor used a different approach, and sometimes different approaches for different trainees.

In Paul's case, one tactic that was successfully used to tap the emotions of these young men was to play upon their attitudes towards women. In 1965, the so-called sexual revolution was just beginning. Couples were openly living together. Sexual intimacy was not delayed until a couple was engaged or married. The values that had dominated the country during the period immediately following World War II were no longer considered inviolable. But most of the boys who enlisted with Paul Reed were quite conservative and respect for women had been a major part of their upbringing. Even the wildest among them expected to be faithful in marriage and to only marry the "type" of girl who would be faithful to them. Yet they also thought of women as the "weaker sex," who had to be protected—like property. A woman needed a man, and many of the youths looked upon dating as something akin to animal mating rituals. The strongest bull in the herd would dominate since the women would go with the most aggressive of the males.

But the drill instructors (DIs) turned that conviction around and suggested that girls were unfaithful tramps. They might seem loyal and loving when they were together. They might even be loyal and loving so long as the boys were in town. But once there was physical distance, the boys were told that their girls could be seduced by the first handsome face, friendly line, and serious offer that came along. Girls would go to bed with any man. The DIs conjured up the image of "Jody," a character from ribald army songs which in other circumstances would have only elicited a chuckle.

Jody was everything their girls wanted in a man. He had the looks to excite them, the money to show them a good time, but most importantly, he was there and available. Jody wasn't a patriot. Jody did not and would not enlist in the army. He had no sense of patriotism, no sense of honor. He was out for a good time and shunned his duty to his country. Jody was everything they were not, and he was taking their women.

The drill instructors' words were reinforced by the events of the day. One or another of the recruits would be having girl problems just as he would have had if he stayed at home.

Adolescent relationships that seem to be solid "forever" are fickle under the best of circumstances. Eighteen-year-olds are a deeply emotional but highly changeable lot, and their commitments are often less than they fantasize. However, many of these youths had no frame of reference other than what their leaders told them. They were in a closed society with little experience in nurturing interpersonal relationships with the opposite sex. Soldiers going into combat needed an angry edge, and this was one way to get it.

Most of the breakups the youths experienced with the young women they were dating would have occurred whether or not they had gone into the service. The relationships were over, and the separation caused by the boys going into the army only made it easier for the girls to send the letters containing messages they otherwise would have delivered in person. A few of the breakups were caused by girls who had been highly dependent discovering that they did not need a steady boyfriend to survive. They sought new jobs. They went to college. They moved to a new community. They did not want to feel emotionally encumbered by someone who had no sense of their experience.

And always there was the reality, apparent though never stated to the men, that Jody could not exist unless the girls let such a man into their lives. Girls were not weak. No one is seduced against his or her will. An affair involves two people, and the girls who had them deliberately went after the men. So each time any of the trainees received a "Dear John" letter, he showed it to his friends. Eventually, many of the youths came to believe in and hate Jody in whatever form he took in their lives.

Jody was mentioned on the firing range, and the young men hit the targets more often. Jody was mentioned during combat training, and the youths became more aggressive. Jody was the focus for anger and hate. Jody was the enemy, and the young men were spurred on by their desire to destroy him.

Then this hatred was refocused on Victor Charles.

Victor Charles ("Victor Charlie" in military parlance stands for VC, which in turn stands for Viet Cong), or Mr. Charles, or Sir Charles was the name of another enemy, this time not a human being. He was neither man nor animal, and could also be called a "gook," a "dink," or a "slopehead." The creature was humanoid in appearance. It walked upright on two legs. It had two arms, and the general configuration of the body seemed similar to ours. But there were telltale signs of the differences.

Gooks were short. The female gook, who could be quite beautiful in appearance and highly sensual when coupling with a human male, was very tiny, often less than five feet tall. The male gook was five-feet-one or five-feet-two inches in height.

Gooks had a method for communication, but it wasn't language. They spoke "jibber jabber." They made high-pitched, almost incomprehensible sounds much like monkeys chattering away at the zoo. They had learned to communicate with each other, though on a much lower scale of development than real human beings.

Gooks had differently shaped eyes and a skin color that was neither Caucasian nor Negroid nor Hispanic. Gooks were rice eaters and could subsist on far less food than was needed to sustain a human being. And gooks were vicious, skilled fighters who would kill you in an instant.

It was the almost superhuman fighting ability of the gooks that led to their being named Sir Charles or Mr. Charles. The instructors who had fought against them respected them and never wanted their charges to underestimate Victor Charles. That certainly included one of Paul's drill instructors, a handsome, muscular, six-feet-tall black man who was filled with hate for both women and gooks, as well as having a compassionate concern for the recruits who would face the enemy he had survived. Many of the young men had seen cornered rats that would leap at a person who had them cornered. A large number of them had gone hunting, encountering the danger of predators such as mountain lions. Victor Charles was all of these things and more because he could think like a human being, plot like a human being, and strike when human beings were most vulnerable.

Victor Charles was not a human being, though. He was incapable of love, incapable of feelings. He might sire young as humans did. And because of their physical structure, the gook females who were not their enemies could bring American soldiers physical pleasure in exactly the same manner as a human female. But they should never mistake a gook for a human being.

Gradually, the anger the young soldiers had developed towards Jody was turned against the gooks. They would be shooting at targets on the range and their instructor would shout, "There's a gook in the bush. He's firing at you. Kill him! Kill him! You'd better kill him before he kills you!"

It was part contest, like shooting alien monsters on a contemporary video game, and part Bogey Man who could haunt the recesses of your mind, convincing you that your worst nightmares could come to life. No one really knew if gooks were quite what they were being told, but they knew from the drill instructors that they were real in some form, that they were frightening, and that they lived in Vietnam.

Soon the idea of killing a gook was as exciting as being asked to go on a first deer hunt. Such creatures were the ultimate challenge.

There was a political side to the gooks as well. They were Communists or tools of communism, though which was never too clear. Somehow, if they were not stopped by American soldiers, other countries—countries with good people—would fall under Communist domination like a stack of dominoes.

Paul Reed was never certain just when he came to hate gooks. He knew he hated Jody after he had a short twenty days of leave before going to 'Nam, which he spent with a former high school sweetheart, a girl he had dated two years before enlisting. They had had fun together, had spent every spare minute together, had declared their love for each other, and had fantasized about their life together when Paul returned.

But soon thereafter, the girl decided they were moving too quickly. She did not feel that twenty days was proof of a lifelong commitment. She wanted Paul to know they should both date others. And when she told Paul she had been dating someone else, was serious about someone else, was going to get married to someone else, he was crushed.

Suddenly, Reed felt he had come face to face with the Jody in his life, and the feelings were so intense that he could still feel the pain and anger twenty years later.

While the hatred for Jody could be traced to one event, the hatred for gooks, the inhabitants of the place called Vietnam, was more gradual. It was noticed first only in flashes, in moments where the idea of hunting a gook, of shooting him along a jungle path, became a fantasy image of great pleasure. By the end of AIT and shortly before the three weeks of paratrooper training at Fort Benning, Georgia, Paul Reed had come to fully hate the Vietnamese he had never met but who were now an enemy worth risking his life to destroy.

Song to Sew Uniforms By
Our soldiers are exposed to rain and sun.
The rain chills their insides; the sun burns their skin.
From cloth we fashion uniforms;
Our soldiers are resolved to exterminate the enemy.
My guy fights zealously on the battlefield;
Your gal swears to give her all.
Be quick of hand, brothers and sisters!
Looms whir, gunfire crackles through the green forest.
We fashion our hatred into poems.
Gunfire rhymes with the looms' whir.
We exterminate the enemy to the rhythm.

> — *A poem in Lieutenant Nghia's diary worded as though written by a sweetheart back home sewing uniforms for the soldiers.*

They were to meet in South Vietnam for very different reasons. Nguyen van Nghia was fighting what was known in his country as the American War. His nation was divided by civil war, the Americans supplying support in the South, and the Chinese, former enemy of Vietnam, supplying several thousand troops to the North.

The war was not a typical one. Traditionally, the people of both the North and the South should support unification of their country, regardless of political ideology. However, the South had a dictatorship as brutal in its own way as that which existed in the North. Moreover, many Southerners were enticed by the prospect of short-term financial gain. Gambling, prostitution, extortion, and other crimes plagued large cities such as Saigon. As a result, many Southern families were deeply divided. Conditions in the South were so chaotic that the government and its economy could not be sustained without outside aid. In 1965, when thirty-seven-year-old Nguyen van Nghia put on the uniform of his country for the second time in his life, ultimate victory seemed most likely for the North. For there was a major difference in perspective between the North and the U.S. Western wars are fought for weeks, months, or years. Israel's Seven Day War is still studied by military historians and tacticians. In Vietnam, on the other hand, wars are fought for generations. An occupation force might last several generations, but each new generation of Vietnamese was taught to resist. Because of their belief in reincarnation, death was not the end of a battle or a war. What was not accomplished in one lifetime might occur in the next or the next. As a result, North Vietnamese soldiers who went South to fight did not expect to return home until the war was won. Many soldiers would be

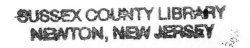

found with a tattoo reading "Born in the North to die in the South" under their arms. They were not on a suicidal mission like the Japanese kamikaze pilots of World War II. But they were committed for the duration of their lives.

Paul Reed knew nothing of the ideology of the enemy. What he understood was the anger of his drill instructor, a man he greatly admired. Because of his strong feelings for the man, Paul Reed decided to emulate him. He would be as devoid of emotions towards women and as filled with hate for the gooks as was his DI. He knew this would earn him the approval of others and would even help him stay alive.

Yet never did Paul Reed have any sense of the enemy as anything other than a nameless, faceless creature. The dehumanizing process continued to be a part of his intense physical drilling as Paul attended paratrooper training in Fort Benning, Georgia.

He was in the best shape of his life. However, it was almost not enough to achieve his goal. The soldiers arrived at Fort Benning around midnight. The sergeant who met them verbally harassed them the moment they stepped off the bus, then ordered them to drop to the ground and do push-ups. He assured them that paratroopers were the army's elite, an infantryman could aspire no higher, and not everyone was going to earn his wings. He bragged that he would get ten men to voluntarily quit the unit before the night was over, then proceeded to put them through rigorous rounds of push-ups and deep knee bends, all with full duffel bags on their shoulders.

The men were soon exhausted. They wanted to drop to the ground, to sleep where they lay. But Reed and most of the others were determined to succeed at all costs. When they witnessed men dropping out—ten in all as the sergeant had predicted—they became even more determined to succeed. Within three weeks, Reed was making his first jump from a World War II cargo plane called a C-119. It had two engines (needing both to stay aloft) and held twenty-four jumpers in two groups of twelve, known as "sticks."

The experience was both terrifying and invigorating. Reed jumped from twelve hundred feet, had his chute pop open, and floated happily towards the ground. The only moment of panic was when he did the unthinkable—he looked down while in his chute. He had been comfortable until then, shifting slightly right and left like a pendulum in a heavenly grandfather clock. But when he looked down, he realized that his feet were standing only on air and that the ground was coming up to meet him very rapidly. Reed knew that the modern parachute was far more maneuverable than in the past, and that it allowed him to drop more slowly. Still, the ground was rising swiftly to greet him, and his feet were dangling over pure air. There was no way to stop other than by striking the ground. For an instant there was panic. Then the training came back—legs together, toes pointed down, hands high on the risers, ready to pull. And PULL! It was an excellent jump.

Later they told Paul that any landing he could walk away from was a "successful jump."

Paul Reed, army infantry paratrooper, was invincible. He was ready to take on the enemy he had come to hate without ever understanding why.

November 1967 found Paul Reed in Fort Bragg, North Carolina, with the Eighty-Second Airborne Division. Although most of his jump school classmates had been shipped to Vietnam, Reed was sent for several months of continuous training in North Carolina. Apparently, the extra men, of which Reed was one, were as yet unneeded. Reed earned an additional MOS (11C, mortarman).

During this period, an airborne unit in Vietnam was reported to be involved in one of the fiercest and bloodiest battles in the "American War." This was the battle for Hill 875 at Dak To, in Kontum Province.

The land was not an objective for the Americans. Unlike previous wars where success or failure was determined by the territory lost or gained from the enemy, the war against the North Vietnamese was tracked with body counts. The more soldiers killed, the closer the army was to victory. And the word "soldiers" could be interpreted in the broadest sense. Since this was often a guerrilla war, anyone might be a soldier in disguise. Accidental civilian deaths of women and children were often added to the body count in order to show success. Death was supposed to be demoralizing, though the truth was that the American strategists had never considered the religious history of the people. Death was a transition, and while the losses were mourned by loved ones who often wanted vengeance against the killers, death was neither actively embraced as the Japanese had done during World War II nor was it feared as was common with Westerners. Had the entire North Vietnamese population been destroyed, the last to die would have believed in ultimate victory because of the battles to be waged in the future by the reincarnated warriors.

Hill 875 was important, not for its strategic position but because a large number of North Vietnamese regulars were on the defensive from within bomb-proof bunkers atop a ridge on the hill just three miles east of the Cambodian border.

The Americans fired into the bunkers and sustained heavy fire in return. Both sides were within grenade-throwing distance, and the battle, which lasted twenty-one days, was ultimately about who could sustain the warfare longer. The Americans hoped that their ability to resupply themselves would enable them to triumph over the Vietnamese, who had to rely on caches stored before the fighting began.

In the end, 285 U.S. paratroopers died and another eight hundred were wounded. Paul Reed knew none of the men, but he knew how they had trained, how they had prepared themselves for battle. Had he been sent overseas earlier, he might have made a difference. He might have been responsible for more of the enemy dead than the almost fourteen hundred North Vietnamese who lost their lives.

Determined to at last see the action for which he had trained, Paul Reed made a request to be allowed to go to Vietnam, one of two he had placed since graduating from paratrooper training and being sent to North Carolina (the first request was denied). This time it was heeded. The American army needed people to replace those killed and wounded. Paul was as good as anyone.

While Paul was concerned with avenging his fellow paratroopers cut down by the deadly gooks, Second Lieutenant Nghia was receiving a different view of the way the war was going. A poem used for motivation was included in the newsletter he regularly received and stored in his rucksack. Entitled "On the Enemy Soil We are Walking," it was printed to celebrate the same battle that so angered Paul, as well as other successes in the field. It was a strong motivator for the men and women, the reason Nghia retained it. Translated, it read:

Who returns to the TRA River?
Who comes to Binh Dinh?
Who stops at the lake?
Who has been in Darlac and Kontum?
Who shall hear the victories everywhere?
The victories everyone knows
Even the rice fields are happily singing for the victory!
The fall will come sooner than later
Open our arms unto the high sky
Hey you sweet country girl. You did help all these victories
Let young men walk faster
Jumping over creeks and through hills to destroy the enemy
Hey, Mom, you got silver/gray hair for this
Mom takes us. It doesn't matter how it is
Mom you give us love
Mom watches us every single step
Even when the wind blows and on chilly early mornings
Mom you give us the energy to get through the mountains
On the enemy soil we are walking
For a thousand years, we still have hope
We stand up as we did at Dien Bien Phu
    [NOTE: Dien Bien Phu is the place where the French
    were defeated]
We sang a victory song once
Even the rows of plowed soil we step on
Even dried hay, stumps, long roads have our footsteps
Even the corners of the inlet know the one present
Even our enemies' high security units, we have been in
Night falls, flames are everywhere in the sky
Shelling goes with the attack. We make damages
We have been angry in our hearts
We attack from many directions, giving the enemy
    no way out

We are stronger than ever
Breaking through hundreds of bunkers
Raise our swords to cut their heads off
Leaving there, are a group of enemy
Here, Da Nang, Hoi An are still fighting
Hien Nhon, Vinh Dien, Ha-Lam, Tam Ky are the same

Oh how wonderful those steps we took
Where the Red River carried so many enemy bodies
Across the hanged bridge walked our soldiers
From Pleiku we come to Tuy Hoa
We sing the victory song for our country
For our entire country celebrates our triumph.
On the enemies' soil we are walking.
We are victorious. We come to face our country.

> — *Poem written by Ngan Vinh, September 1967*

Victory did not mean triumph in the sense that it would for the Americans. Nghia longed for home, for family, for a chance to return to the land, to raise crops, feed his wife and children, and to be the husband a man should be. Tradition held that he should be the person making the decisions, bearing the burden. It was right to fight for the unification of his country. It was right to have to endure the hardships he had too long faced. But he desired to return to the world that should have been his life had the outside invaders not come to Vietnam, had the South not kept separate what should be united.

For seven years I have stood guard at the seven-span bridge,
So many times I have paced back and forth.
Life overflows on the Northern shore
And spreads to the high sea.
Oars splash to the beat of the rowing song.
Why does the South so move us?
On the Southern shore of the narrow river
The nights are dark and lifeless.
I feel the crying of the people.
I have met many sweet sisters on the Southern shore.
Their sufferings find me on the other side of the seven-
    span bridge,
Leaving me ever troubled.

> — *Part of a poem written by a friend of Lieutenant Nghia who had spent seven years as a guard at the famous Hien Luong Bridge, over the Ben Hai River, which separated North and South.*

5

CHAPTER FIVE

P aul Reed and two hundred other young men boarded a chartered civilian airliner on February 21, 1968, for the long flight across the Pacific Ocean. They were traveling to Bien Hoa, Vietnam, and though none of them would ever be the same again, they had no sense of what awaited them. Attractive hostesses brought meals, drinks, smiles, and flirtatious conversation. The cabin chatter was more along the line of what might have been heard if the men were traveling to the Superbowl, not to war. Laughter frequently resounded throughout the plane.

The following day, as the flight neared its destination, the hostesses remained smiling and friendly, but the men had grown silent. They were scared and uncertain about what they would be facing. They knew the landing field could be shelled by the enemy, that snipers might fire at them as they disembarked. They were aware that they were entering a foreign culture; that mingled among the faces of seemingly friendly, supportive natives were men and women armed and planning to kill them. They were away from everything familiar, certain only of each other and the leaders under whom they had trained.

When the plane landed and taxied to a stop, the terror that had been suppressed came to the surface. Paul and approximately fifty other men tried to race to the exits. They wanted to be out of the aircraft, out of range of whatever violence might await them.

The landing ramp was delayed for a few minutes, forcing the still smiling hostesses to stay by the door, not letting anyone leave. Paul felt the intensely hot sun on the metal surface of the plane. Whether because of the closely packed bodies of the men trying to disembark, the sun, or their own fantasies, the heat seemed to rise to intensely uncomfortable levels. He felt like a potato wrapped in aluminum foil, baking in an oven.

When the doors finally opened, the men heard their first sounds of warfare. From somewhere in the distance they recognized small arms and mortar fire. They knew it was not a training exercise, yet they had no idea if the shooting was close enough for them to race for cover. When they saw that everyone on the ground was ignoring the distant sounds, they tried to relax. They did not want to appear as naive as they were.

Later Paul was told that the airport had come under heavy attack a few hours earlier. This shelling by rockets and mortars happened on the same day they had left the United States. But in Vietnam, you quickly learn to ignore what is not an immediate danger. Paul was different in attitude and appearance than he had been in basic training, but he was like the other men new to Vietnam. His body was lean and hard. He felt ready to tackle any physical challenge. Yet he had the baby face and virgin eyes of a youth who had seen horror only in a movie theater, not in real life. He had yet to encounter the extreme atrocities one person can commit on another, had yet to have to look in a mirror and see the face of someone who had been committing some of those atrocities. Although he wanted to be accepted as an experienced veteran, he had no sense of what real experience could do to a man.

It was Jeffrey Ratzlaff, a friend from the United States, who gave Paul his first glimpse into what lay in store for him. Ratzlaff had been in Vietnam for several months, fighting with the First Brigade of the 101st Airborne Division. The last time Paul saw him, he had seemed to be just another teenage man/child in basic training, a dedicated youth concerned more with girls, drive-ins, and cars than with war. Now everything had changed.

Ratzlaff had been issued the same military clothing and equipment as Reed. But where Reed's boots were spit-polished black, Ratzlaff's boots were brown and rough, with their soles coming loose. They had been through too many streams, rivers, monsoon rains, and muck that seemed to grab a man's leg and try to hold it in place. The humidity was intense, and even with the harsh, hot sun, nothing ever dried.

Reed's friend was also exhausted. His eyes had circles under them, evidence of long periods with inadequate sleep. He needed a shave. He needed to eat more regularly. He had aged well beyond his years.

And Ratzlaff was healthy compared with a second man Reed met that day.

The second man was at first drawn to Reed's silver wings which identified him as a paratrooper. The stranger's uniform patch indicated he was from the same unit to which Reed was being assigned. Though he was at the end of his tour of duty. Paul was just beginning.

Although it was obvious that Paul was airborne, the man asked Reed's unit's name. Then, upon hearing it spoken aloud, he froze. His eyes seemed to glaze over, then widen in horror. He looked like a member of the cast of one of the science fiction movies so popular when Paul was dating. They were usually shown at drive-in movie theaters, and they frequently involved creatures such as giant ants or monsters released from long-term hibernation. The first sighting often resulted in some actor playing the role of a citizen driven insane from hysteria. He would briefly be seen running down the road or being forced into an asylum where he would be heavily sedated after telling what he witnessed to the police or military.

The soldier's eyes looked like those of the actors playing such roles. He was also angry, his lips quivering as he spoke. Paul sensed that he was scared, hurting. He said little, then momentarily received the focus of the odd man's wrath: "I just hope you like killin', cause you'll get to do plenty of it where you're headed."

The man left, and Reed realized that the veteran was just as damaged as if he had received a gunshot wound to the stomach. There were those who would physically die in battle. And there were those who would mentally die from the stress of battle, though their physical bodies would remain functioning for what might be a half century or longer. This man was as much a casualty as if he had lost his limbs or his life.

Reed believed he was stronger, was certain he would not let his emotions destroy him. But he also realized that war was more than training yourself to fight, to kill, to survive at any cost. Something more was happening to men in battle, something he had not experienced, was not certain he wanted to experience. He reminded himself of why he was there, of the fact that his country needed him. Yet there was an uneasiness that had not existed before.

Paul was surprised to see so many Vietnamese women on the base. They were young and attractive, like perfectly sculpted, tiny china dolls, but Reed knew that they were really female gooks. They would never be quite human in his eyes. He had been trained too well. If women in general could not be trusted, how much less so female gooks. The hatred that he had picked up in advanced infantry training had become second nature to him.

But Paul wasn't thinking back to AIT now, he was looking forward. He just wanted to belong to the men who were fighting. He wanted them to see that he was a part of the effort, new to Vietnam, perhaps, but still adequately seasoned. He even went so far as to roll in the dirt to look "not so new" before going to the mess hall to have his first meal in the land where he would fight and friends would die. The effort was wasted, though. Everyone who saw him had either played the game or had friends who did. The old timers jeered and laughed at him. Paul hated the feeling.

The 173rd Airborne Brigade was less tolerant of what they called an NG ("new guy") than were other units. The 173rd had been created from remnants of a World War II unit, the Second Airborne Battle Group of the 503rd Infantry. In 1963, they had trained for jungle warfare on the island of Okinawa, where they developed an attitude of elitism as though they were a special unit, like the Navy Seals. They developed the nickname "the Herd," and the bugler summoned them to reveille by playing the theme song from the television western series "Rawhide."

It was May 5, 1965, when the men of the 173rd were sent to Vietnam as the first U.S. Army combat unit to be put in place. By the time the war ended, they were one of the most decorated units of the war. Among the fighting men were a dozen Medal of Honor winners. Others earned thousands of Purple Hearts and eventually over six thousand Bronze Stars. Reed had a better chance of surviving combat because he was in the midst of men who had seen so much action. But as a new guy, Reed made the old hands uneasy. He did not know how to survive in real warfare, how to keep from endangering the others.

The 173rd ran a school meant to familiarize the incoming troops with life in the jungle—a sort of on-the-job training. The students were taken out on day and night patrols and ambushes. They learned to read a compass and a map of the terrain. Reed trained on the PRC-25 (Personal Radio Communications-25), Claymore mines, Lightweight Anti-tank Weapons (LAWS), the M-60 machine gun, and the M-79 grenade launcher. He and the others also learned about the insects, many of which were unusually large. They joked that the mosquitoes could carry off a fully loaded soldier. This particular discomfort had to be endured because insect repellent and other protective chemicals could be smelled in the bush by "Charlie." The men also learned that the malaria pills they needed to protect themselves from the disease carried by the mosquitoes caused diarrhea which could strike while on the patrols. This sometimes meant walking long distances in their own filth, unable to stop or change clothes because they would be too vulnerable to the enemy.

Poisonous snakes were everywhere. Later on in his tour, when the men of Paul's platoon were all lying on the ground, taking a break, a green bamboo viper slithered right across the leg of David Harman (one of Paul's friends). There were 133 different types of snakes in the areas where they would be on patrol, 131 of which had venom that could kill. The vipers were the most frightening for Reed. Because they were just two feet long, slender, and light metallic green in color, they blended with the foliage in the bamboo thickets, becoming virtually invisible to anyone passing by. They could drop unexpectedly and strike at will. The snakes were all different, but were referred to by the common term "three step." A victim would only be able to stumble three steps before dying.

Among the other snakes were the kraits, which stayed on the ground and could be avoided by watching your step. However, if they were accidentally stepped on (even if wearing boots), they could snap their front half into the air, twist their heads, and fill an ankle or leg with poisonous venom.

It was all an alien world for a Texas teenager whose life had been on the city streets and in the suburban malls of Dallas. But Paul was determined to gain the approval of the other men, of the officers, of his drill instructors who had prepared him for battle. He finished jungle school, thinking only of the enemy he was there to kill, not the hardships and dangers of his living conditions. He willingly took his M-16 and began packing the tools of his trade: an olive-drab rucksack on an aluminum frame, the basic equipment of Claymore mines, mortar rounds, body bags, ponchos, poncho liners, up to five days of C-rations, four canteens of water, a flashlight with red lens, a personal transistor radio, batteries, writing paper, pen, and a small album of pictures from home. Most men carried the pictures because looking at them was a positive reminder of life back in "the world." They were an incentive to win battles and stay alive so the soldiers could return.

Paul was sent to Kontum Province as a replacement soldier, a term he had never carefully considered. He was assigned to A Company of the First Battalion and made the short trip alone in a Caribou, a lightweight cargo plane capable of using very short runway space. Arrivals and departures from Kontum Province made use of a "cold" portable airstrip, known as PSP (perforated steel plate). The landing strip was nestled in the midst of rolling mountains and hills which were in every direction, and thus was not under attack.

Paul had fantasized about this moment, when he would join a group of men, tough, primed for the fight, heavily armed, flawlessly prepared, marching with their heads high, uniforms as flawless as if they were on parade, destroying every gook in their wake. The reality was quite different. Paul didn't yet know that he had taken his last bath for more than a month, but he did learn quickly that he was not seen as someone special—he was a body. A Company had lost a man. Reed was there to fill a hole. His presence might assure success where, without him, battles would be won by the enemy. Even if he didn't turn out to be much help, at least he was another target for the bullets. If truth be told, the veterans hoped that the New Guy's presence would assure that they would not be killed, that the New Guy would intercept the bullet with their name on it. An old timer's life was worth more than that of a New Guy.

The men of A Company met the tiny plane in full battle dress, including camouflaged steel-pot helmets. They mostly wore ammunition bandoliers strapped across their chests, and adhesive tape was used to keep the magazines and grenade pins quiet. Several also wore belts of M-60 machine gun ammunition, and everyone had knives strategically placed on their bodies for fighting and survival.

The men were not spit-and-polish. They were filthy, their unshaven faces covered with caked-on sweat. Their eyes were set back in their heads, their expressions a mix of wariness, exhaustion, and disdain for the "NG" who had nothing to offer the battle-hardened unit. Reed was disappointed until he learned that two days earlier they had joined with C and D Companies to fight an NVA force of unknown size fairly close to where they were standing. Seven of their men were killed, two were missing in action, and twenty-four more were wounded.

War is an activity of the young. Those who survive into old age understand the dangers. Only the young still feel invincible, still can believe that no matter what else happens, somehow they will survive.

The "old man" of A Company, commanding officer Captain Jim Davis, was a slender man with a ruddy complexion, a little taller than Reed. He was twenty-six or twenty-seven years old, originally from Texas, polite and caring about the men. Frequently referred to as "Diamond Jim Davis," he seemed an odd man to be a father figure, yet again Reed knew that he would do his best to win the captain's approval, wherever that took him, whatever that demanded.

The NG was assigned to Oscar Platoon (one of four platoons in the company), whereupon the veterans immediately began breaking him in. Several of the men removed mortar rounds and some other pieces of equipment from their rucksacks, laying it on the ground beside his. Reed was expected to lighten their load, becoming the platoon's pack mule as his initiation. He was expected to carry approximately double the normal load. Nothing was said about the extra weight when he was ordered to load his gear and move out.

The men moved in single file, approximately fifteen feet between each man. In the lead was the "point man," who led them in the direction of the enemy following a grid coordinate on a map or orders by the commanding officer to go to a pre-specified position. The point man was always alone, always alert. Generally, he would be the first target for a sniper's round.

It was not fear of the enemy that drained Reed's energy so much as the humidity. The sun was intensely hot, the humidity so high that sweating seemed impossible. He stayed wet—wet from rain, wet from sweat, wet from urine, or wet from blood.

Sometimes it was his own, sometimes it was someone else's; but he stayed wet. Neither flesh nor clothes ever completely dried, an environment that led to jungle rot, crotch rot, foot rot, and all kinds of rot. The dampness would cause minor cuts to become severely infected within hours, creating a festering poison that could kill a man if he failed to get it treated. New men were given penicillin, but the problem was so pervasive that, after someone had been treated several times, he would develop an immunity to the antibiotic. Ultimately, very high doses of tetracycline had to be used, and even these were not always effective. Once, while changing his socks (as he did every two weeks or so), Reed noticed that his toes were webbing together like those of a duck.

A rifle was a constant hand-held companion and was always held at the ready. Men learned that the thickness of the jungle and the nature of the warfare was such that shooting might begin before an enemy could be spotted. Even slinging an M-16 over your shoulder could mean fatal additional seconds before you could return fire.

The war was being fought by the clock. The Vietnamese understood the terrain better than the Americans. They could move about at night with relative ease. The Americans would establish a base camp perimeter each afternoon at three o'clock. An 81mm mortar was placed in a freshly dug pit in the center of a circle of protection. The pit had to be twelve feet in diameter and two feet deep. Then sandbags were filled and placed two and three layers deep around the upper edge of the pit. The thirteen-pound rounds of ammunition were stacked within easy reach of the weapon, and the pit could also be used as a refuge from shrapnel and incoming bullets during a firefight.

Other foxholes were also dug, though these were used solely to protect the men. They were six feet deep, six feet long, and two feet wide. Sandbags stacked four levels high were at each end, and three six-foot trees were located nearby, cut, and placed lengthwise on top of each foxhole. Then two additional layers of sandbags were placed on top of the trees. The work resulted in a crude bunker that still could save your life. The men who had been in the field longest liked to sleep on top of the bunkers so that they could roll off into the protected foxhole should shooting start. New men favored the mortar pit until they learned that it would fill with water in even the gentlest rain.

Most of the men lived in hooches at night. A hooch was little more than a poncho stretched horizontally between some trees and tied with string so that it was about two feet above the ground. Each of the four ends were secured; the men then slept or sat under the stretched-out poncho and wrote letters, ate their meals, or listened to transistor radios with earphones when they weren't on guard duty. Snakes were always a danger. Insects and leeches made their way onto their flesh. But most of the rain stayed off their bodies—a simple pleasure that most Americans take for granted.

Meals were a mix of C-rations and LRRP (long-range reconnaissance patrol) rations. The choices included turkey loaf, pork slices, beanie weenies, ham and eggs, scalloped potatoes, and others. Everything was meant to sustain adequate nutrition while in the field, and the men soon developed their favorites, trading with the others.

A field stove was made from an empty C-ration can and a small amount of plastic explosive taken from a Claymore mine the men would break open. The heat warmed the meals, a luxury in the midst of the humidity.

When night finally arrived, the darkness was total. It was like being totally blind. No matter how carefully planned earlier combat training had been in trying to simulate combat conditions, nothing could prepare a city boy for the complete lack of any light. The glowing tip of a cigarette could be seen from a great distance, permitting a sniper to zero in and fire from far enough away to avoid his own detection. Any light, no matter how slight, was a danger.

While some of the Americans stayed on guard, the rest slept—fitfully if at all. The night belonged to the enemy. Accustomed to the jungle and the night, they were able to lay mines, set booby traps, and dig pungi pits (holes in which excrement-topped sharpened sticks were placed to cause injury and infection to the unwary who stepped or fell on one). The NVA frequently could infiltrate the immediate area of the camps, and sometimes passed through the guarded perimeter.

The only time the methods changed was when Captain Davis decided to set up an ambush. Just before total darkness, seven or eight of the men would be sent a short distance from the perimeter along a well-used trail (called a tango). They spread out at arm's length, just off the trails, then lay on their stomachs, their eyes focused straight ahead, their M-16s under their arms, ready to be fired.

Each man was expected to stay alert for ninety-minute watches; those not on guard duty tried to rest as best they could. Watch was changed by the man who was coming off watch gently placing a wristwatch in the palm of the hand of the next man. Although sleep was allowed for those not actively on watch, most of the men remained awake all night. Fear of snakes and tigers and the discomfort of mosquitoes was too much for resting.

It was March of 1968 when the dangers of war became most apparent to Paul. He had endured the discomforts all men and women suffer in unfamiliar jungle terrain. And death had become familiar. Exploding mines, booby traps, and snipers had begun taking lives of men he knew. Reed's attitudes towards the Vietnamese were hardened. "I hate him ('Charlie')," he wrote to his parents two weeks after a Vietcong guerrilla action where several planes were bombed and blown up in what the Americans thought was a properly guarded ground area. "I really do, but I'm keeping my cool. I only hate him because I cannot possibly love him. It's not my job while I'm over here to 'love thine enemy.' I can believe in that when I come back to the world. Yeah, I can't wait either.

"But don't worry Mom & Dad, I'm keeping my head down and my rear a little lower and reading my Bible and saying my prayers every night. I know I won't go to hell. God will say I have been in hell and remove me. God is good."

It was also in March that Paul Reed and Nguyen van Nghia "met" for the first time, though neither was aware of the other.

The conflict began on the afternoon of March 16, 1968. Paul Reed was in a Special Forces camp named Poli Klang, a tiny, secure outpost in Kontum Province. He was to be a part of a helicopter combat assault on an area controlled by the NVA.

At 3:00 P.M., American artillery units began pounding the proposed helicopter landing zone with high-explosive shells. The idea was to kill or drive out all the enemy soldiers who might otherwise ambush the arriving infantrymen.

Once the firing stopped, the helicopters loaded with Paul and his fellow soldiers flew in tight formation just above the treetops. They were accompanied by two gunships which tried to discourage any snipers near the landing zone.

The men were ordered to load their weapons, putting a round of ammunition in the chamber so they could shoot the moment they left the helicopters. Oddly, the act of becoming fully armed seemed to relax the men, who knew that takeoffs and landings were the times during which they were most vulnerable to attack.

The helicopters never completely touched down. There was high elephant grass, and the pilot misjudged his elevation. Instead of being four feet from the ground, as the men expected, they dropped eight feet, falling onto each other.

The enemy had fled as they had hoped, though there was evidence that the area had been occupied not long before. Approximately a hundred rucksacks had been recently abandoned, an action that meant they had no time to plan.

Reed was one of those who volunteered to go out and reconnoiter the area, gaining as much information about the enemy as possible. One by one, moving ranger file, they went down the east side of the mountain. The trek was slow and tedious. The trees, thick brush, and steep slope made moving difficult. The high humidity made the men feel as though they were inhaling water with every breath. Their body strength was ebbing as they moved, a fact that scared them since they knew they had to be ready for any action.

The jungle was silent, an experience the men found frightening. Birds should have been singing. Other jungle noises should have been heard. They did not know if the silence was protective in the midst of these intruders, or if there were already others in hiding, rifles aimed, booby traps set, death just one more step away.

Suddenly Reed saw personal items and trash so fresh that the Vietnamese had to be nearby. There were small bottles, papers covered with writing, and other items. From what he had heard about other encounters, it seemed likely that they had found the belongings of men who had been observing the 173rd's position. He reached for the items only to have his hand slapped and be reminded that "That's gook stuff; leave it alone."

Before anything could be said, the men emerged from the thick cover of the trees and gunfire erupted. Grenades exploded all about them. Small-arms fire struck the earth and the trees. There was no way to tell the direction from which the enemy fire was coming. They were caught in the open and had no way of knowing where to go to reduce the chance of being cut to pieces. They were facing superior firepower and the element of surprise was in their enemy's favor.

Reed and the others dropped to the ground, listening to the mortar shells, firing wildly, moving as rapidly as they could for cover each time a round exploded. Every few seconds there would be a scream, a cry of "I'm hit," or "Medic! Medic!" But there was no way to help anyone until the firing stopped. Reed (and the others who could) made their way to the cover of the trees.

There was an abrupt silence, and in moments those who were able began moving towards the wounded and the dead. Bleeding was profuse, yet they began hauling them back up the mountain to the safer perimeter. Ten were wounded, several with obviously serious back wounds.

Other units had identified an NVA bunker position, and soon Reed joined with D Company for a counterassault. However, while the Americans traveled on the land, the NVA had been digging tunnels between massive tree roots. Artillery, air, and napalm strikes were almost useless. Even worse, when a confrontation between ground forces was imminent, the NVA soldiers used ropes to climb to the high limbs of surrounding trees. When the Americans rushed the area where they had been in hiding, the NVA snipers began shooting from their high position.

That afternoon Reed experienced war as soldiers had always known it throughout history. The weapons had changed, automatic weapons fire replacing the clash of swords with shields. At times the enemy was no more than twenty meters away, a distance smaller than some Dallas parking lots. Everyone heard the other soldiers chattering away with each other and they knew that it was a matter of killing everyone or being killed.

Finally, darkness descended and the Americans withdrew. All they knew for certain was that one of the enemy soldiers was dead, along with five of their own men who were originally thought to be missing in action. Another seven were wounded but alive. In addition, C Company had their own encounter with snipers, experiencing a two-hour firefight that left seven North Vietnamese soldiers and one American dead.

From My Heart of Hearts
The enemy guns thunder
More madly with each passing moment.
Marking the fall of many of my friends;
They will never know life again.
The motherland weeps for them.
How can we possibly surrender?
We are the proud soldiers of the bridge,
Bearers of the Party's teachings.
We must silence the enemy,
Still them like glassy waters.

— *Poem in Nguyen van Nghia's diary*

17/March/68
Sunday Aft.

Hi Mom and Dad,
. . . We are on a big mountain North of Pleiku about thirty-five or forty-five miles, getting ready to go up the next mountain beside it which is about twice as high, except for one problem, there are NVA at the top, in bunkers waiting for us. For three days now, we have poured artillery, napalms plus 750 lb. bombs, mortars everything, and a few of them are still there. See, if you're dug in about six feet underground, about the only thing that will bounce you out is a B-52 bomb raid. B-52s mean death…

Before they went to the top of that mountain they took their backpacks (we call rucksacks) off and left them, just like we do before we go up a steep mountain. Well, A Co. sent out a patrol and found fifty-two of these NVA rucksacks, which we so smartly carted back with us when we left. When we got them back we searched them. They had in them: TNT fuses, mortar rounds, clothes, documents, ponchos, books and cans of rice. The rucksack I searched had an NVA regiment flag, a

*North Vietnamese newspaper, some Communist litera-
ture, TNT, a VC flag, some clothes, can of rice, a blue
sweatshirt, which they all had, a brand new pair of
scissors, and a picture of his wife and little baby, two
North Vietnamese stamps, and a letter. Well, Captain
Davis let me keep the NVA flag, the scissors, the newspaper, the letter, the pictures, and the stamps.*

*Needless to say I'm keeping them as souvenirs
and I'm going to send them home soon. Also, this
pack contained some American carbine M-1 rounds,
like my M-1 fires and a can of U.S. oil. I believe this
was an officer's pack because of the Communist lit-
erature, handbook, and documents. He also had
fuses for the TNT, and some grenades, and some
Cambodian batteries.*

*Most of the other packs, contained a lot of U.S.
made goods, like ammunition, blankets, grenades and
just anything they can get their hands on.*

*This man has a cute child and a pretty wife, but I'm
sorry to say that they will never see him again. Once
the 173rd finds them, they get tracked down until they
are no more, it's as simple as that. In a way I feel sorry
for him because he don't really know what he's fighting
for. Old Ho Chi Minh has him brain washed, but he's
my enemy, and too bad for him…*

—Paul Reed

It was 4:30 A.M. on March 17, and Reed could hear a firefight to
the southeast. A group of NVA soldiers had overrun a base that
was supplying mortar support. At the same time, the Fourth
Infantry firebase to the west was overrun, every man was killed,
and all artillery pieces captured. Then Captain Davis noticed a
large number of NVA soldiers moving north and east of their
position, using flashlights and torches to light their way.
Although the lights revealed their presence, they also indicated
a force so large and trying to move so quickly that their leaders
were certain they would be able to overrun the Americans who
were still on safe ground.

The commanding officer quickly radioed for support from a
plane nicknamed "Puff, The Magic Dragon." This was an old

C-47 specially outfitted with what was called a "mini-gun" protruding out the rear door. These special weapons, powered by an Emerson electric starter motor, had six rotating barrels much like the Gatling gun, the original machine gun of the old West. Placed on maximum fire, the guns fired over six thousand rounds of 7.62mm NATO bullets every minute, saturating an area the size of a football field with a bullet every three square inches—no living being could escape. Every fourth bullet was a tracer round, and the bullets were fired so rapidly, the tracers gave the appearance of a continuous light, like a bright red laser beam dropping from the sky.

Reed and the other Americans were protected by setting a special strobe light inside their perimeter. It was specially shaded so it could not be seen by the enemy, but the bright white flashing light was easily visible from the sky. The plane would avoid shooting at the area immediately surrounding the strobe light position.

The use of Puff changed the course of the battle. Whoever survived the bullets fled the area. Then another company used helicopters to send the Americans on an offensive maneuver against the NVA soldiers who were still attacking the mortar base. By around 8:00 A.M., the NVA were in retreat, moving into yet another company of Americans who fired three hundred mortar rounds at distances of less than fifty meters from the defensive perimeter they had established.

As the different units fought, the ones not under fire were able to locate a cache of explosives and ammunition. They found an area the NVA were forced to abandon which contained twenty-three 82mm mortar rounds, forty-one 82mm fuses, fourteen hand grenades, and 580 rounds of semi-automatic ammunition. Both sides were prepared for prolonged violence.

At 6:00 P.M., with the light fading fast, Lieutenant Doane (November Platoon leader) and Captain Davis prepared a new approach for what they knew would be continued fighting. The NVA knew that the Americans never move at night. Once they establish a protected perimeter they stay within it until daylight.

The NVA also were aware that when their position was located, as it had been during the firefight, artillery strikes would be used against them throughout the night. The logical strategy for them would be to move from the base of operations they had used during the day, abandoning for the night the bunker complex that the Americans had located until it was safe to return the next morning.

Lieutenant Doane proposed that a patrol be sent out to sneak into the NVA bunker complex, reconnoiter the area, return and lead the rest of A Company into an ambush position. When the sun came up and the NVA returned, they would face an unexpected ambush.

The patrol went out at 11:00 P.M. Six men were involved, three of whom would stay at a nearby river and wait with the radio. (The radio, however, was kept turned off since a radio breaking squelch at night could be heard for miles.) The other three, including Lieutenant Doane, who had the original idea for the attack, moved another seventy-five yards up the hill before the lead man, Steve Charbonneau, stopped. He had found a hole in the ground with a bamboo lid on it. He foolishly slipped his hand inside, forgetting two important points. The first was that the object he encountered was a latrine (which became obvious after he thrust his hand inside and felt something moist). The second was that the NVA always place such latrines just in front of their bunkers. There was a good chance that he was leading the other two into an occupied camp.

The men traveled twenty-five meters more, facing a thickening of bamboo and other foliage, which added to the darkness. Then they traveled an additional twenty-five meters, most of the time having to rely on senses other than their sight, crawling on their hands and knees.

Suddenly, Charbonneau stopped again, this time realizing the mistakes he had been making since he discovered the latrine. He could hear a gook asleep in a hole in front of him. The breathing was even and noisy enough so that the danger was unmistakable.

Charbonneau, having whispered his discovery to the lieutenant, again placed his hand in a hole. This time he found not a latrine, but a sleeping gook. When he reached in, he accidentally awakened him. But rather than attack, the NVA soldier was silent, unmoving, probably as terrified as the American who had discovered him.

The Americans were in the middle of a bunker complex. The NVA must have thought they were friendly troops. Certainly, they had no reason to feel anyone had discovered their presence. Lieutenant Doane immediately concluded that he had been as wrong about the NVA relocating their position that night as the North Vietnamese soldiers were mistaken about the Americans never sending out night patrols.

The three men moved another ten meters before an enemy machine gunner began firing. All the NVA soldiers were instantly awake, grabbing their weapons, and firing wildly. No one knew who had invaded them, how many were there, or in what direction they were located.

The lieutenant and the other two Americans immediately started running. They dared not attempt to return gunfire for they had not been spotted. The muzzle flashes would have let the NVA see them for the first time. Instead, the men used the light from the enemy weapons to show them the bunker openings. They tossed hand grenades into them as they fled, the delayed explosions of the grenades keeping them from being spotted.

It was only when the six men were together that they began returning fire. The three men who had waited by the water had stayed in their position rather than risk being killed by an unknown force. This kept them all alive, and when they saw an opportunity to flee, they radioed for the 81mm mortar platoon to begin firing on the enemy position as the Americans returned to their base.

Paul Reed was one of the Americans who monitored the radio and began working the fire mission. The men worked quickly in the dark and fired the first round immediately. Capt. Davis saw through his field glasses that the round exploded short. Corrections were sent to the plotter and another round was fired. The second mortar round was quickly followed by a slight adjustment and within seconds a third mortar round was on its way. It struck the enemy's ammunition storage area, limiting their ability to return fire and probably killing any man who was nearby.

Fifteen more mortar rounds were fired before the enemy grew silent. The NVA had either fled, died, or been wounded. Fortunately, Lieutenant Doane and the five men under his command returned safely, but a little sheepishly. The thinking about how the NVA would handle the aftermath of the first day's fighting was mistaken and it had almost cost him his life.

Fighting continued throughout the day. The Americans began advancing. The NVA, though off balance, fired back with mortar rounds and snipers. Patrols and ambushes were established, then sent out repeatedly.

It was one of these patrols which found the base camp Lieutenant Doane originally thought the NVA had retreated to during the night. The bunker area had nothing to do with the camp, and Lieutenant Doane had been right in his thinking after all. The problem was that the base camp was so well hidden by trees, brush, a swiftly moving stream, and hills nestled between two mountains that no night patrol could expect to find it.

Paul Reed was among the men who were sent to check out the NVA camp. They started far enough away to be able to study the camp with field glasses without being seen. The place seemed generally deserted.

Suddenly, an unarmed enemy soldier appeared. He spotted the Americans, turned, and started to run. One of Reed's friends leveled his M-16 and fired several rounds into the enemy. Reed happily told himself, "That gook is history."

There was no return fire. Either the camp was empty or they were now on the alert, waiting.

Reed and the others moved cautiously forward into the base camp. It had not been deserted long because Reed's nose detected a very distinct odor which could be found anywhere there were NVA soldiers.

Men in the field have long been taught how to survive in whatever wilderness they find themselves. In the land that is now Israel, ancient wilderness dwellers lived on locusts and honey, both of which were plentiful. American soldiers fighting during World War II received instruction on the edible plants and animals of the European and Asian locations where they would be fighting. It was not unusual for a man to have to make a meal of a wild rat in order to stay alive. So it was for the North Vietnamese soldiers who found themselves in familiar, yet enemy-held land. Fish was plentiful in the streams, but time to catch the fish was not always available. They needed to use every part of the fish that was edible, including the heads, and so they combined rotting fish heads and gooey rice, making a foul-smelling concoction called *mam sac* (which means "stinky fish stew"). American GIs mistakenly used to call it *nuoc mam*. *Nuoc mam* is a much more palatable fish sauce which can be found in even the finest Vietnamese restaurants. Actually, the concept of *mam sac* was not much different from the original use of chili in Reed's native Texas. In the nineteenth century, Texans would mask the taste of spoiling beef with a blend of ripened chili peppers, beans, and other less perishable items. Sometimes this blend, the forerunner of contemporary chili, made them a little sick. At other times the mix was relatively harmless, the chili peppers raising a man or woman's body temperature just enough to fight the bad effects of the beginning spoilage. No one ate that early Texas chili unless they needed it to survive, and the same might be said of the *mam sac* used to sustain the men in the jungle.

The smell of *mam sac* was unlike any Reed had ever encountered. It was foul enough to make him nauseated, like the rotten-egg smell of sulfur dioxide gas. That fact, coupled with the fear as each step took them further into the unknown, forced Reed to fight down a compelling desire to vomit.

The only other camp smells he would encounter both that day and in the weeks to come were those of opium and marijuana, which permeated the NVA base camps. Drugs were a too-common relief from fear, loneliness, and isolation for soldiers on both sides of the war. Many Americans and NVA soldiers thought that marijuana was less dangerous than alcohol and no more addictive than cigarettes. Reed declined to use either.

There were tunnels around the base camp—a gook subway system in Reed's estimation. They were so small that Reed could barely insert his head. There was no way he could wriggle into any of the openings.

Again the size helped dehumanize Charlie. Only a nonhuman could fit into the tunnel system. They were like giant, humanoid gophers. They had to be.

The men kept creeping closer, constantly on the lookout for a trap. They had made noise killing the lone soldier they encountered. If the base was occupied, it was also ready for them. Still, even in their fear, they wanted to see the layout.

There were hammocks strung between trees for sleeping. There was a kitchen area where such field "delicacies" as *mam sac* were prepared. Weapons and ammunition were stored in a third location, and a hospital was set up in another corner of their grounds.

Reed found the organization fascinating. Mountainside embankments were used, and steps had been made with the commonly found moist black dirt. The steps went up the mountainside to enable them to have high ground advantage as well as an easier way to travel quickly. The steps were fashioned from the black dirt and were as dry and hard as concrete.

The engineering feat surprised Reed, who had thought the NVA incapable of such sophisticated achievements. He climbed them to see if they would crumble, but instead of falling, the steps held, and he and the others discovered fifty-two gook rucksacks filled with equipment and personal items. They were captured spoils of war, their owners either dead from Puff and the other fighting, or soon to die. They had abandoned the rucksacks in order to move quickly, as the Americans would do, then planned to return for them. The terrain was such that no one would find them except for those who owned them, so leaving them behind was a help when attacking.

The rucksacks were searched when the men returned to their base. In one there were two flags—an NLF (National Liberation Front) flag used by the Vietcong, and the other the unit flag for the NVA 304th Division. There were other things as well, but Reed was especially interested in some orders and an ID card. Although much could not be read by Paul, the name seemed legible. It was Nguyen van Nghia.

"I hated him. I knew that much about him. I hated him. And I hated all of them just like I hated him. He was just somebody I was trained to hate," Reed would later remember.

The captured items were treated like a stack of toys bearing nobody's name: All of them were placed as in the midst of small children who have been told that the toys are for them and they must share. Everyone understood what they were expected to do, yet everyone also wanted to keep as a souvenir whatever he found most precious. The VC flag was especially in demand, even by Captain Davis. Reed eventually ended up with a rucksack, a diary, and a few other odds and ends, including several pictures of happy young Vietnamese women's faces. Reed kept the items, with Davis's approval, and made plans to ship them to his parents for safekeeping.

Later that day, Reed and the other men linked up with D Company and marched north-northeast towards the area known as Hill 1064 on their maps. A valley with high ridgelines ran parallel along the east and west sides of the mountain. That valley was covered with head-high elephant grass and bamboo thickets, part of a jungle area that was under a thick canopy of foliage.

The NVA had turned the hill into an elaborate fortress. The slopes were laced with carefully constructed, effectively camouflaged bunkers and trenches, all spiraling downward among large trees. They had been built several months earlier, so they were covered with natural vegetation rendering them nearly invisible from both air and ground. Each was designed so that soldiers firing at an approaching army would not risk endangering their own men.

There was a honeycomb of bunker connectors so that when one location was spotted and attacked, the men could move to a different, equally well-protected location. It was a perfect setup, and when D Company led the initial assault, seven men were killed almost immediately in the close gunfire.

Reed's A Company came under mortar attack as the men moved up the north flank. The shells were exploding everywhere, and many of the men became so terrified that they tried to move into the area where they thought the next ones would land just to end the nightmare. A wound—any wound—would earn a "dust off" ride in a medical evacuation helicopter. Death was also a possibility, of course, but even that was preferable to the psychological assault of the shelling. It was as though they had been set in the center of a corral where they were to be slaughtered. But instead of their killers moving in and shooting them, an ever-tightening wall of bullets made them watch their deaths inch towards them. There seemed no escape, no relief from the horror of the impending destruction.

The chances for survival were better at Hill 1064, but the men were often too terrified to think about possible escape. The flanking maneuvers of the attacking Americans kept them in positions from which they could be pulled back. When Captain

Davis realized how deadly the enemy's position was for the ground forces, he gave the order to move back while artillery and napalm support were brought in. The Americans descended while the rounds of ammunition from the big guns went whistling over their heads, exploding so close that if any round fell even a few yards short, it would have meant death by "friendly fire."

Reed closed his eyes to pray just before a twisted piece from a 155mm shell landed less than three feet away from him. The shell had exploded on target, one twisted piece of red-hot metal ricocheting back down the hill. It landed harmlessly, though Reed slightly burned his fingers when he instinctively leaned forward and touched it.

Night was fast approaching and the men were ordered to dig in where they were on the hill. Normally, they would have had a fallback position for nighttime, but nothing had been prepared. They had not expected the sophisticated fortress-like setting nor the intensity of the resistance they encountered.

The slope of the hill was at least forty degrees and the men had to remain in a prone position to keep from rolling. Some stayed on their bellies and tried to dig foxholes with their shovels. They made some progress, though it was a little like trying to dig with a spoon. They could not get the leverage to move fast enough and deep enough for effective protection.

Reed and a few others crawled to large trees. They could prop their feet against them, lie prone, attach their bayonets to their rifles, and be ready for anything.

The darkness, when it came, was total. No one, American or North Vietnamese, could see the others. Two men could be side by side and never know it. None of the Americans was carrying food and few had water.

No one slept that night. Several times Paul was certain he heard the enemy approaching, certain he heard them come within a few feet of where he was braced. It was likely that they were probing the perimeter, but like the Americans, they could not see anything in the total darkness. No one fired their weapons. No one shouted a warning. The silence was as enveloping as the blackness of the night.

By morning Reed was stiff and exhausted. He had not been able to tell the passage of time, only that for too long it had been dark and suddenly he could see a bit of his surroundings.

On March 18, stiff, sore, and worn, the men moved up the hill without meeting any resistance. There they found seventy-five foxholes and a half-dozen dead NVA. There were also several mass graves indicating that the number of dead was far greater than the men left behind.

The remaining NVA had vanished, apparently having left under cover of darkness.

That night the men settled in on the top of the next mountain over. They had high ground cover from an assault, but nothing could protect the men from a skilled lone sniper. Suddenly, Daniel Burr, one of Reed's close friends, had a single round of ammunition pass through his chest. No one had seen the sniper. No one could tell from where the bullet had come. One moment Burr was alive. The next moment he was on the ground with a sucking chest wound that would collapse his lungs, create massive bleeding and infection, and kill him slowly.

Burr was dragged to a foxhole and one of the medics grabbed some clear plastic taken from around the radio batteries they had with them. He used the plastic to seal the chest wounds, hopefully prolonging the soldier's life until he could get proper medical treatment.

"I'm going home," said a delighted Burr. He was in good spirits, having no awareness of the seriousness of the wound. He also did not know that he had gone into shock, his body shutting down the pain receptors so he could not feel the horror of what he had just endured.

Reed tried to comfort him, desperately holding back tears. He knew his friend was going to die. He knew that there was nothing he or anyone else could do. The sniper had found his mark and now his friend was going home, though not the way he believed.

A helicopter's blades could be heard in the distance, but Burr was not comforted. The shock was wearing off, and he began to gasp and scream in agony.

The helicopter started to land when another gunshot rang out, this time passing through the chopper and wounding the pilot in the foot. The pilot instantly pulled up and left the area.

Angry, the men began returning fire in the direction of the sniper. What they did not realize was that despite their high position, they had been surrounded. It was only when another chopper pilot approached their position from the opposite side of the mountain and was also shot at that the soldiers learned how precarious was their situation.

Daniel was fading rapidly. Reed held his hand, trying to comfort him, at the same time shooting at the enemy and tossing fragment grenades in the area where he thought they were hiding.

Daniel, fighting the pain, again said he just wanted to go home to his family. There was no hope, though. He died holding his friend's hand.

It was with the death of Daniel Burr that Paul Reed developed the hardness and anger he had so admired in the drill instructor who first introduced him to the world of Mr. Charles and the gooks. The creatures had brought death into his world in a manner more intense than anything he had experienced before. His letters home would take a harsher turn as well.

> *...We assaulted two hills and every time the gooks would see us coming, they would get up and run. We just mowed them down...After we left there weren't no trees in sight—ha ha. Two gooks even tried to surrender. Sorry 'bout that. They bit the dirt. Everybody made a big joke out of it. We're all kill crazy anyway, I have to admit. It was a little fun and Vietnam is the only place you can shoot at people and be authorized to do it. We found two wounded gooks in a foxhole. I myself wouldn't have killed them, but someone else did.*
>
> *We took three prisoners of war. They interrogated them all night. These were NVA. After it was all over, we policed up the bodies, twenty-seven of 'em. It was a terrible sight, but to keep from getting sick, I had to laugh out loud like everyone else was doing.*
>
> *Mom, don't worry about anything, but you know what war does to a man. I'm getting bloodthirsty just like all those other airborne rangers, and the only NVA or VC I like to see is a dead one. That means so they can't shoot back.*
>
> *— From one of Paul Reed's letters to his parents*

The battles within Kontum Province were the most intense Paul Reed would experience. On March 20, A Company was searching the area of Hill 1064 when one of the men, taking a break, managed to put his foot through an opening in the ground. It was a cave in the side of the mountain. It had been covered with logs, then covered again with dirt. It was concealed so well that it would probably have been missed in a deliberate search.

The cave held a cache of fifty 120mm mortar shells, twenty-four 122mm rocket rounds, twenty-six 122mm rocket warheads, and several unidentified warheads, all in their carrying cases. The men were ordered to pack it all downhill to the landing zone D Company was creating. From there it would be helicoptered out.

The rocket motors—six feet long and eight inches in diameter—were both awkward and heavy. The men were exhausted trying to take them back down the mountain. They were amazed by the stamina and determination of the Vietnamese soldiers who had carried them on their shoulders all the way from North Vietnam.

For the next three days, all four of the companies which were part of the joint operation of the First Battalion made contact with NVA troops. Air and artillery fire were mixed with direct contact. American casualties were relatively light, but the men knew that such a blessing could change at any time.

The change came on March 26 when the point man walked into an ambush, an AK-47 round striking him between the eyes. The other platoons immediately flanked the enemy position while Reed and his friends put out a steady stream of weapons fire against ten heavily armed snipers dug into positions between fifteen and twenty meters away. Artillery support was impossible because it couldn't penetrate the density of the tall trees that provided so much cover. The gooks prevented A Company from retrieving the body for nearly three days. Reed's anger burned deeper.

"Between firing, I could hear gooks chattering gookese back and forth," Reed later remembered. "We were screaming at each other, too. I know they heard us…all I wanted to do was kill gooks."

Paul's parents read his letters in horror. They knew he could be shot, maimed, killed. They understood that he was now in a situation where they could no longer help him, advise him. The love they had given him over the years, the morals they had tried to teach him, all meant nothing on the battlefield. Perhaps God would bless him. But perhaps God was blessing all the young men, those who would come home to find jobs, marry, raise children of their own, and those who would end their lives thousands of miles from anything familiar. Perhaps God was even blessing the North Vietnamese.

What shattered Paul's mother was that the army had taken her son from her in ways other than physical. He had been taught to hate, and in hating, he had crossed some invisible line between childhood innocence and the adult knowledge of hell.

He had to hate in order to kill, she would later explain. She understood that in theory. What she did not realize was how far he would go, how much the death of the man whose rucksack he sent home would be the blood of his own soul. In order to win the war, the fighting was not only destroying the enemy, it was destroying the young men who had been sent into battle. None of them would ever return. In their place would be youths who had seen too much, done too much, destroyed all they once held precious and dear. She knew that no matter what the Vietnamese were like, they were not so horrible as to be worth taking a gentle, slightly rebellious but happy child and turning him into a man who could delight in taking a life.

The battles in Kontum Province continued throughout the month before A Company was moved to Bong Son in Binh Dinh Province. The NVA had been forced to slow their attempted takeover of the highlands. Both sides had sustained extensive casualties. And Paul Reed sent home a box of souvenirs which would remain unopened and forgotten for the next twenty-two years.

6

CHAPTER SIX

Few warriors remain heroes very long after returning home. There may be a parade or a memorial. There may be requests to talk before an occasional civic group. There may be questions from wide-eyed teenagers wanting to live vicariously through the battlefield experiences of the neighbor boy who has just returned from overseas. But the warrior quickly learns that no one wants to hear the truth. They want to hear their fantasy of the moments of glory and none of the reality of the horrors that are a daily occurrence. No one really wants him to talk about the truth of what he did and witnessed.

War is about death. War is about pain. War is about destruction. The youth who has engaged in combat has helped commit unspeakable violence on whichever people have been deemed the enemy of the moment. It does not matter if that means the Egyptians or the Jews, the Greeks, the Romans, the Germans, the Russians, the Japanese, the Koreans, or the Vietnamese. It does not even matter if that means one's own people, as occurred in the American Civil War. There are actions that must be taken in times of war that are so horrible, no one wants to admit that they could love the men who committed them. Parents do not want to hear their sons talk of the victories that resulted from destroying some other mother's son. Politicians do not want to be reminded that they authorized the teaching of a generation to hate so much, they would willingly do to others what, if it occurred within their own land, would result in the person being locked away from society for the rest of his life. They also do not want to be reminded that the body bags were necessary only because of the violence those same politicians declared too patriotic not to endure.

Even worse are the unspoken questions. Can you stop hating? Can you stop killing? Did you like taking a life? Did you like having the blood of a stranger on your hands? Do you no longer know any other way to deal with others?

"It's over," the soldier is told. "Get on with your life." The GI Bill which enabled World War II veterans to go to college and buy a home was a way of telling the soldiers "We're proud of you. Now shut up and get to work on living your life in the 'real world.'" As a result there were many veterans suffering from stress for a generation or more after their service. Heart disease and other problems occurred disproportionately among those who saw combat compared with other men their age who spent the war stateside or otherwise away from combat zones.

When assessing the stress of combat on Vietnam veterans, it is important to remember that, as in most wars, only a small percentage of the men and women who were stationed in Vietnam ever actually encountered the enemy. Even at the peak of American involvement, no more than one soldier in eight, and probably no more than one in ten, experienced the terrors of combat. Most spent their days in an exotic Asian city with unusual food, attractive women, and low-priced souvenirs they could ship home. They were scared at times. They were lonely. And they were aware that other soldiers were returning wounded for life or in body bags. But the violent confrontations were somewhere in the distance, almost always unrelated to their lives.

There was unusual anger in America when Paul Reed returned home from his tour of duty. Soldiers who once would have been respected for the service they gave to their country were ridiculed for not trying to beat the draft. Hostility toward the war cost Lyndon Johnson the White House and forced Richard Nixon to make ending the war a priority of his administration. Yet none of this really much mattered to Reed. Instead, he was haunted by the changes.

Like most men who experience combat, Paul Reed had as much trouble adjusting to civilian life as he once had adjusting to the military. The bedroom of his home offered inadequate means of escaping if the enemy attacked. He would drift off to sleep listening for the sounds of enemy footsteps. He would instinctively sniff the air for smells that would warn him of enemy bunkers. His sleep was always light, and he was uneasy being barefoot and in pajamas at night. You couldn't fight in pajamas. You couldn't fight without your boots. For months he had been taught to never let himself be vulnerable to anyone, to be prepared to flee, to hide, or to fight and kill. Suddenly, such behavior was inappropriate. He was home, safe, surrounded by loved ones, and he didn't know how to handle the experience.

There were other problems as well. The more he distanced himself from the war, the harder it was to admit to some of the acts he committed while in Vietnam. For example, there is a cultural side to any war, and Vietnam was no different from the earlier wars of history. The American Revolution pitted the British, who wore colorful uniforms and expected to confront their enemies like gentlemen—face to face and man to man—against the colonists who often fired from ambush and then ran away. The colonists had become guerrilla fighters as a result of the terrain and the tactics necessary when fighting the natives. They were held in disdain by the British, whose overwhelming military force would undoubtedly have been victorious with conventional tactics.

During the French and Indian War, the Indians were taught to scalp their victims after they were killed. This variation on the body count used in Vietnam was proof to the Europeans that the Indians helping them with the fighting were making the impact against the enemy that they claimed.

In Vietnam there was another cultural issue. One facet of the war was the attempt by all sides to create fear and hurt morale. There were religious issues of reincarnation that were part of the Vietnamese belief system which the Americans soon learned. According to the thinking of many in the North and the South, a person had to die without any form of body mutilation in order to be reincarnated or eventually go to heaven. Even an autopsy, so standard in the United States, would be in violation of their religious philosophy. As a result, it was routine for many of the Americans (along with both the North and South Vietnamese) to cut an ear off each enemy soldier they killed.

The idea of mutilating a corpse was more horrible to some Americans who did not experience the war than the idea that people were being killed. They could not grasp the psychological significance and how it might reduce the enemy's fighting spirit when this happened to fallen friends. Yet Reed and others in the midst of repeated battles came to enjoy this tactic.

It was best for the men to remain silent, to limit what they told. Unfortunately, over time this meant that the veterans began to look upon themselves with loathing, forgetting the context of their actions. They had acted in the manner they felt was necessary to stay alive. In theory they could share such experiences with other veterans of the war, but few would do so. There was always the fear that there would be condemnation even within the community of Vietnam vets.

There were other problems as well. Reed had seen horrors which few Americans ever experienced. Rape victims, anyone who loses a child in a traffic accident, from illness, or as a result of crime, and others who experience extreme trauma never truly heal, never forget the moment of loss, the horror of what will never be again. Combat veterans are similar in that they might be able to lead rich, full lives, but a part of them never fully heals from the nightmares they have witnessed.

Paul Reed, like many other veterans, did not try to seek help for his problems. He had never heard of post-traumatic stress disorder, never been told that difficulties with adjusting to civilian life after combat experience were normal, not something akin to mental illness. In fact, at the end of World War II there were jokes about civilian readjustment. One story that widely circulated was about a marine who was being sent home. "A group of ladies are having a tea party. You've been asked to join them. How will you enter the room?" And the marine answered, "I'd take out my .45, roll in a grenade, and come in firing." That joke was heard in 1945. The 1970s would be no different.

Reed married almost immediately after leaving the service. He was twenty years old, intensely lonely, haunted by a world he had never known existed, and the young woman said she was in love with him. He thought she would bring him peace and happiness—poor motivations for a wedding. Within four years they were divorced, having recognized that they were together for all the wrong reasons. Reed attended college and married a second time four years later. This marriage was stronger, both of them more mature. Still it did not work, though a son was born of the relationship. That son, Silas, an answer to prayer, was the delight of Paul's life, and when the couple divorced, Paul obtained sole custody, his former wife having regular visitation rights.

Still troubled by the normal confinement of city living, Reed became a long-distance trucker. He routinely traveled from coast to coast and up into Canada from his base in Weatherford, Texas. The pay was excellent, the work forcing him to keep his mind focused on something other than the memories of Vietnam. Yet something was becoming very wrong. Trucking, he realized, was a way to stay in physical and emotional isolation from others. He was also irrationally angry, sometimes experiencing deep sadness and other times severely depressed. He was troubled by the fact that none of the feelings seemed related to what was happening in his daily life.

Paul did not realize that he was suffering from post-traumatic stress disorder (PTSD), in part because it was unfocused. His life had changed little, and what change there was seemed to be for the better. There should have been no reason for the mood shifts, the anger. Still, he was able to work, to love his son, to raise the boy without too much difficulty. Thinking about what was happening seemed counterproductive. Reed simply put the issue from his mind (a practice that veterans commonly call "stuffing it").

It was Independence Day in 1989 when Paul Reed took a friend to the Cotton Bowl to see the annual Fourth of July fireworks display. Paul arrived during the early evening hours and saw a large display near the front gates. It appeared to be a stack of red Texas granite blocks on a plywood platform, and as the two of them approached it, he saw hundreds, perhaps thousands of names. To his amazement, the names were part of the Texas Vietnam Veterans Memorial that would officially be dedicated on November 11 of that year—Veterans Day. Reed did not try to read the names, looking for friends who had died in battle, as some of the visitors were doing. Instead, he suddenly became overwhelmed with a wide variety of emotions. He felt his chest constrict, as though someone had sat on him, hindering his breathing. He gasped for air, and as he did so, he realized that tears were streaming uncontrollably down his face. Humiliated, he ran from the crowds of people, not knowing where he was going, what he was doing, or why.

Some people say that when you die, your entire life flashes in front of you. Unfortunately, the only ones who could confirm this are dead. But if true, then Reed's experience was the opposite. His Vietnam experiences raced through his mind, both shattering his emotions and freeing him in a manner that would eventually lead to a new, less troubled life. He felt intense grief, heartache, anguish, sadness, guilt, and feelings of loss. He could not focus on any thought, any feeling. He was unable to express what was happening, even to think in a logical way. It was like experiencing a videotape that revealed the deepest aspects of his being, not just an audio/visual record of the past.

Paul Reed did not realize it, but the time for healing had come to him. In the next several hours and days, Reed was a living newsreel, seeing events from his time in battle in a manner he had not previously experienced. Some were old memories he had thought about over the years, such as the post office signs recruiting volunteers with a picture of Uncle Sam pointing at the patrons, the caption saying, "I need you." He remembered the television nightly news coverage of the early years of the war. He remembered seeing people dying, though in a dispassionate way, much like watching a war movie on television. He remembered the newspaper articles, remembered protesters saying that too many people were dying, and he remembered the politicians talking about the "domino effect."

Reed still hated the Vietnamese, no matter for which side they had been fighting. He did not leave the hatred behind in the hills, valleys, and mountains he had spent a year traversing. He carried it over against the refugees who had settled in Texas as well as second- and third-generation Texans whose ancestry once had been Vietnamese. He had killed and wanted to kill some more. He liked the idea of having his enemies die. He felt he had saved yet another American with each passing dead man, woman, or child. He hated equally, without regard for who the individual might be.

Reed had also been isolating himself from the issues of war and peace that affected international commerce and trade with Vietnam. He did not want to think about the people and their children. He just thought about killing, something he once could do as easily as sip a cold cola drink on a hot day.

Then came the memories of events he had so long suppressed, he was troubled by having to live them once more. He thought he had recalled the horrors in which he participated as a young soldier, but too many had been put from his conscious mind in the time that had passed since he left the military.

After experiencing the war memorial, Vietnam became the primary focus of Paul Reed's existence. He was obsessed with seeing old newsreels, documentaries, and discussions. He was drawn to movies and television shows which so much as mentioned the war. His parents were concerned, uncertain what they could do to help him. Finally, his mother recalled the box he had shipped to them from Kontum Province, a box that had not been opened by anyone in over twenty years. Some of the contents Reed remembered. Others were long forgotten. When his mother suggested he open it, hopefully letting the souvenirs ease his troubled mind, he decided to try it. "I remembered them saying, 'If something doesn't kill you, it can heal you,'" Reed said later.

Opening the box was like peeling back what little scarring had covered the psychological wounds of the past. Memories came to the surface like the festering pus of an infected wound as he looked at the pictures of his enemies, the writing, and other items. He did not look too closely at first. Just the sight and smell of the contents of the aged rucksack were enough to trigger too many bad memories.

Some of the images that came to his mind were of friends who had been brutally massacred in the midst of combat so intense that Reed and the others had to retreat from their positions without removing the corpses. By the time they could return to the damp, hot jungle area where the men had fallen, nature had rapidly decomposed their bodies. Maggots slowly moved in and out of now hollow eye sockets. Flesh was bloated and rotting, like spoiled, overcooked chicken. Foul-smelling meat would fall from bones at the slightest touch. The stench of escaping body gasses filled the air.

Even two decades later, the memory of those corpses renewed his anger. Hatred for the enemy of his youth burned within him. The men of A Company had killed the Vietnamese in the same manner, and the friends of their enemy had had to abandon them to the identical conditions. Yet to Reed, only the enemy had been the barbarian, and he wanted revenge.

The box represented piles of North Vietnamese whose lives he had helped destroy. He recalled the time his company was sent by helicopter to repel a North Vietnamese attack against a U.S. Army convoy.

Their arrival at the location had met with no resistance. Then, as they assaulted the enemy positions, several of the enemy panicked and ran. Others stayed in foxholes so hidden that they were able to fire at the backs of the Americans as they moved past. Several of the Americans were hit by the AK-47 rounds before they could respond.

Paul remembered someone screaming, "There they go! Get 'em!" He saw two North Vietnamese soldiers running towards the treeline, quickly had them in the sight of his M-16, and fired. They were not lives. They were targets no different than what he had shot on the firing range. This time, though, the bullets tore flesh, muscle, and blood from the human "targets," who were dead almost the instant they hit the ground.

Reed remembered being delighted with the sight. He recalled their last gasps for breath, recalled how much fun it was to see his enemy suffer momentarily, then drop.

Reed remembered checking the treeline again, remembered seeing two more Vietnamese. They had lost their will to fight, their hands in the air to surrender. They were boys, no more than sixteen or seventeen years old. They were frightened, war having become as real to them as it became for Reed

when he reached Kontum Province. Reed had been strengthened by the battles, determined to triumph. These boys were
different. They wanted to live without more death. They did
not know that their action assured that they would never see
their loved ones again.

Paul Reed, the soldier, had no interest in taking gook prisoners. He fired off three more rounds, felt the recoil of the
weapon, watched them drop.

The boys had killed his friends, and if they hadn't, there
would come a day when they would. Let some other mother
weep that night. He wanted them dead.

Then he remembered the ritual of stacking the dead. The
Americans would drag the corpses of their enemy by the arms
and legs, handling them much the way deer hunters handled a
fresh kill. Some of them were malnourished and so small that
their bones were brittle, snapping under the stress like dry tree
branches. All of them were stacked in piles of fifteen to twenty.

Some of the men were missing body parts, especially heads
that had been blown off or mutilated beyond recognition. Paul,
like the other men, had snipped off a few ears, both to upset
their comrades who would know their friends had no chance
to be reincarnated to fight again, and to have some souvenirs.
Then he unbuttoned the fly on his pants and urinated on the
dead bodies. It was the ultimate disrespect, a final way of vent-
ing his hate, perhaps of disguising the fear that was a constant
companion to which no soldier dared admit.

When the work was done, the souvenirs taken, Reed remembered being so hungry, he placed a can of C-ration peaches on
the chest of one of the corpses and began eating. Captain Davis
walked by, looked at him, and said, "Are those your peaches?"
Reed said they were, delighted with the feeling of total victory.
Had he been asked to burn the corpses he mocked, he would
have been delighted. However, mass burial was the preferred
method for destruction, and a bulldozer was soon brought in to
dig a hole, then shove the corpses into the ground.

With the opening of the box, the corpses returned to the
surface of Paul Reed's mind. He could see the flesh exposed by
destructive bullets, the half heads with exposed brains, gore,

and chunks of skull. He could smell the rotting carcasses blending with the sweetness of the peaches he had eaten so long ago. He could see the mouths of some of the dead opened in soundless screams, and on others who had been shot in their sleep, expressions of peacefulness.

It was all there, as though recorded on a videotape. The images filled his waking moments and populated his night-mares.

At first the box seemed to have some special powers. Open it and the memories came flooding in. Close it and there was momentary peace, a respite from hell.

Over the next few days and weeks, opening the box helped Reed desensitize himself enough to begin thinking, begin heal-ing. Soon he could leave it open all night without the artifacts slipping into his dreams.

With the easing of the emotional reaction, Reed was able to look more closely at what he had found anew. There was money, a pair of scissors, envelopes, North Vietnamese postage stamps, a card on which had been printed a copy of a military marching song, an ID card bearing the name Nguyen van Nghia, photographs of several people, and a small brown book. Everything was well preserved, though the only item that interested Reed was the book, which appeared to be a diary. It was written in Vietnamese.

Reed looked at the pictures, trying to decide who each per-son might be and what their relationship to Nghia might have been. He identified Nghia readily because of his military rank insignia. Reed also saw that a photo of a boy sitting on his mother's lap must be a picture of Nghia as a child. Another showed him with his sister while still young. And another was that of his pretty wife.

As he stared, Reed realized that he was looking at images documenting the entire life of a gook. They were all that was left. The man had died twenty years ago.

There was something about seeing the photographs that was troublesome to Reed. He wanted the owner to be a gook like the ones he remembered pulling into piles. He wanted him to be little more than an animal, a creature of no consequence.

Yet this gook had carried pictures to remind him of his home life just as Paul and his fellow soldiers had often carried pictures of their loved ones.

Days passed and Paul Reed became obsessed with the little brown book. Studying it helped him put his life in better focus. He remembered when he first realized he was suffering from post-traumatic stress disorder. He remembered when he first started being inexplicably angry.

He recalled the flashes of hatred and fear that took him to the edge of irrational violence. He read about others who had experienced the same reactions, from soldiers to rape victims. Each might have had their own unique trauma, but all of them shared a loss of innocence, a loss of a portion of their previous lives.

For the first time in two decades, Paul Reed questioned not only his past but his training. Were the Vietnamese his enemy? Was the anger necessary? Should he have been taught to kill?

Too many questions.

Like his mother, Reed understood the necessity of building anger into a soldier in order for him to stay alive. He understood the necessity of having him so comfortable with the thought of destroying his enemies that he needed to be able to fight without hesitation. And he understood his mother's asking if she had lost him when he lost his innocence on the battlefield of Kontum Province.

Reed purchased a Vietnamese/English, English/Vietnamese dictionary and began the laborious process of translating the diaries. To his frustration, his lack of knowledge of grammar and sentence structure left him with a set of meaningless words.

Then he went to a Vietnamese restaurant in Dallas. He approached the owner, showed him the book, and let him read some of it. The man did, quoting a little—too little to be meaningful—but not wanting to be bothered with serious translation. He did not have the time, he explained. He could not be bothered.

A friend published a newsletter for Vietnam veterans. An advertisement placed in that paper brought four responses, but all proved ineffective. One supposed translator never got started on the project. A second never finished.

Finally, he received help from another friend named Jill Ewing. She worked with a man named Vinh, a Vietnamese man she found friendly and willing to translate the material.

However, Vinh was from South Vietnam and had served in the ARVN (the South Vietnamese army). He and his family had been the targets of the North Vietnamese aggression to reunify their country. He was uncomfortable with the diary because of his hatred. Several weeks after being given the book, he said to Reed, "This guy enemy and it hard to read what he write. I hate him."

Vinh had to translate it. Reed was desperate by then. He needed to read the words of his enemy. He needed to know the man whose possessions had been captured as spoils of war. He needed to gain whatever understanding was possible. Vinh had to reconsider.

Finally, after much pleading, Vinh reluctantly agreed. The language was a variation of his own dialect and the translation would be slightly crude, but he could give him a close approximation of what was written.

Vinh was troubled when he again saw Paul Reed. He hesitantly explained that the enemy was a "good person."

Reed was outraged. "Good person?" he roared, again remembering the corpses of his friends.

"Yes," said Vinh, unable to find the English words to explain what he had found. "He even family man."

Vinh had to be wrong. In a sense, he was a gook, too. After all, he was from the same country as Nghia. But Vinh had been living in the United States. He was Jill's friend. He was changed somehow. He was more human. He was…

It didn't matter. Reed knew Vinh was mistaken. There was nothing in the diary that could change the image of Nghia as the creature who had haunted his days and nights like all the other soldiers of the North.

Paul began reading the diary. The translation was crude as Vinh had explained. But the words were ones he should not have seen, words like mom, dad, soldier, civilian, enemy, wife, children, and most of all, the word "love." Even more unsettling was the fact that the writing was poetry. Love poetry. Love of country. Love of friends. Love of family. The poetry was of loneliness and fear, of anger, duty, hope, and regret.

Day after day Reed read the translation. He looked at the photographs. Sometimes he closed his eyes and imagined who the people might have been in the life of Nguyen van Nghia, the "dink" who died at Kontum and whose rucksack he had taken.

Gradually, the hate seemed to fade and he could see the pictures for what they were. There was the little boy Nghia, perhaps four years old if Paul could base age on how his own son had looked when that small. The boy was happy and safe, being cuddled in the protective arms of his mother, who obviously loved him deeply. The picture radiated the same warmth and joy as photographs he had seen of himself in his own mother's arms at the same age.

Then there were the references to his mother:

Spring is here; your son yearns for
His mother and native village.
Buds burst to greet the new year;
Love spreads as the blossoms smile.
Spring is here.

Paul had had similar feelings, and he had been gone for just one year in Vietnam. This man had been gone for seven years with no sense of when he would be home again, whether he would ever see her in this life.

There was a poem of love for his wife, filled with frustration at being in the midst of a civil war in which his enemy was no different from himself. He longed to return home, yet felt he had to do his duty. He was a soldier and he could not rest until his mission was over. Still, he would not lose heart because of his love.

I Cannot Wait in Vain
My darling, I can't take this anymore.
I only know my little life.
A diamond reveals its full worth
When shining in the darkness,

Inflaming sweet happiness.
I only want to hear poetry as the sun sets;
I promise I will be loving, faithful.
Our laughter will ring out in every direction.
I only want to watch the autumn sun set,
Your heart beating next to mine.

Our renewed life will arrive on the morning wind,
Once the clouds pass by.
I only want a pleasant autumn.
Love is forever and never forgets.
I will receive your love with open arms,
You are a beautiful flower at age twenty.
I only want your heart to belong to me.
Though we all too briefly shared love
It gives me reason to live.

Paul Reed wasn't married when he went to Vietnam, but he recognized, in the words he was reading, a man whose heart was a mirror of his own. His enemy was a soldier first and foremost. He loved his country, loved the men with whom he joined to fight a common enemy. But he was also a gentle man, someone who cared deeply for his family, for his wife, for his children.

There had been a custody battle over the primary care of Paul's son following his divorce. For many reasons, Paul had been allowed to raise his son, to have the boy live most of the year with him. Much of the healing that had taken place was because that boy touched the gentle side of him, broke through the barriers the army had tried to place over his heart. And here was a man who had seen far greater combat than Reed, had experienced many times the horror, letting the diary be the link to the same intensity of love that engulfed Paul Reed each time he held Silas in his arms. It was like looking in the mirror and discovering that if the flesh could be stripped away, all that was left would be identical. The enemy did, indeed, have a soul, and it was that of Paul Reed.

The realization was too emotional for Paul. Just as he had been taught in the military, he tried to drive the healing thoughts from his mind. Instead, he remembered the war as it had been. He would close his eyes and see himself on ambush, lying in wait for the enemy.

Ah, one approached. He would draw a bead, gently squeeze the trigger. The shots would ring out, three rounds, perfectly placed.

"Die, you zipperhead!" Into the water, the lifeless hulk whose blood floated on the surface, then dissipated into nothingness.

That was truth. An enemy was an enemy.

Except...

Gradually, Reed was able to get more of the diary translated, along with the other materials he had captured. Nguyen van Nghia had been born and raised in Tay Giang commune of Tien Hai district, Thai Binh province, near Haiphong Harbor, eighty miles southeast of Hanoi. He graduated from the military academy in North Vietnam, and was commissioned a second lieutenant assigned to the 304th Division of the People's Army of Vietnam (PAVN), an elite unit assigned some of the most difficult fighting of the war.

The men of the 304th Division took the same oath to serve their country as Paul Reed took to serve his own. They carried military marching song cards to recite as they marched south down the Ho Chi Minh Trail, the link between the North and South.

Reed read the translation of the newspaper Nghia had carried and found it quite similar to the American *Stars And Stripes*. He realized that he had not been fighting a rag-tag guerrilla force who happened to get hold of sophisticated weapons. The NVA were surprisingly worldly men who carefully planned and executed their attacks. This was an army as worthy of respect as his own. This was a soldier with whom Paul Reed would have been proud to serve.

Gradually, Paul Reed realized that some of his military training had, in part, been a lie. None of the men understood the enemy. If anything, it might be argued that there was no enemy except as they were told there was one. The people of the North wanted to unify their nation and go home. They didn't want to fight the Americans any more than they wanted to fight the French or the Chinese before them. They certainly did not want to fight each other. But they had been called to duty and they responded with their lives, just as Paul and the other men of A Company had done.

The feelings of hate seemed to ease. There was still much anger. There was still much that was irrational about the way he was thinking. Yet Nghia was dead, and the diary that had been left behind needed to be honored through Reed's forgiveness of his enemy. He realized that if Nghia were still alive, he would want to thank him for starting the healing process more than two decades after the war ended.

CHAPTER SEVEN

Paul Reed talked about the diary of Nguyen van Nghia with David Rodriguez, a counselor at the Dallas Veterans Center. Another man, Dale Doucet, who was living in Louisiana, suggested that Paul might wish to return the book to the family. With the war long over, it was again possible for Americans to travel to North Vietnam. It would not be difficult to locate the survivors, since Vietnamese families do not move much at all. Perhaps the journey would help the healing process. During this period, some journalists and a documentary photographer also became interested in the story.

Reed was not yet ready to let go. He wanted Americans to understand him. He had been trying to explain the war, his actions, and the feelings when he was in college and to various civic groups who were interested in hearing him.

Paul tried to be truthful, not realizing that someone who had not experienced combat could not understand what he was saying. "I did someone else's dirty work," Reed would tell people. He explained that he had been young and naive, as were most of the soldiers. They were manipulated by the recruiters, the drill instructors, and others. They were to be pawns in a killing game where the manipulators were the odd couple of uninvolved politicians and survivors of the war to which they were sending more young men at risk of dying. "We took pride in the job we did and advertised it on our helmets. We wrote 'LBJ's Hired Killers.' We thought the words carried authority: 'Hey, man, don't mess with me. I'm doin' LBJ's work.'"

Despite that, despite the fact that he was one of many, Paul Reed wondered what possessed him to go along. Some of it was the patriotism of a gung-ho kid of eighteen who knew life only in terms of black and white when the reality was very much gray. Certainly, he believed President Kennedy who, before his assassination, was escalating the war involvement from eight hundred men to twenty-five thousand in order to contain communism in Vietnam. He said that if Vietnam was Communist dominated, the rest of Southeast Asia would fall like dominoes standing on their edge in an endless, precarious row.

Sometimes Paul risked telling what it was really like to be dehumanized while a soldier. He mentioned watching a mother come upon the corpse of her freshly killed Viet Cong son whose ears had been cut off. She stared for a moment, then in a high-pitched bloodcurdling scream she shrieked over and over again, hysterical and on the verge of madness. She was a Buddhist, and the American enemy had just assured that the man/child she had carried in her womb, breast-fed, nurtured, and deeply loved, a youth who was a patriot for his country, would neither be reincarnated nor allowed to reach heaven. He had been forced into an eternity in limbo, a fate too horrible to contemplate. And Paul felt nothing about her grief over a youth who otherwise might have tried to kill him. She was a curiosity, perhaps a little humorous or odd to watch, but that was all.

These were not the feelings of the boy who had enlisted in the army. These were not the feelings of the father for whom Silas was the joy and stability of his life. These were the reactions of a soldier who had been taught to put his humanity, his compassion, and the ability to love on hold.

Sometimes Paul tried to explain how completely comfortable the men became with violence after a few months in. He had been given a few days R&R (rest and recreation) in Hawaii six months into his time in Vietnam. His family flew out to meet him, yet no matter how much he wanted to see them, he was uncomfortable the entire time he was in what the others thought was paradise. He had become a stress junkie. The constant rush of adrenaline caused by facing life or death situations on the battlefield every day had become as addictive as

Paul Reed at Fort Bragg in June 1967.

Paul on patrol
in Kontum
Province,
March 1968.

Paul, hanging a mortar round, about to fire during the battle for hill 1064,
March 1968.

Capt. Jim Davis, Paul's commanding officer, is on the left. This photo was taken during the battle for hill 1064 in March 1968. On the right is Raymond Carpenter, Capt. Davis's RTO (radio telephone operator).

Paul, taking a break one day after the battle for hill 1064.

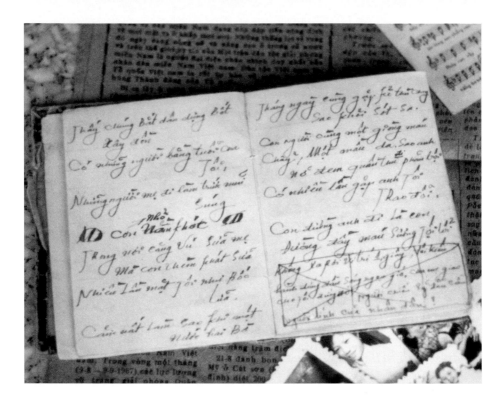

The Diary in Second Lieutenant Nguyen van Nghia's rucksack, captured by Reed's unit during the battle for hill 1064 in March 1968.

Some of Lt. Nghia's photos that were captured along with his diary.

For several years, Paul thought that this was a photo of Lt. Nghia. Actually, it is one of Lt. Nghia's friends, believed to have been killed in the war.

An NLF (National Liberation Front) flag, commonly referred to as the VC flag, which was in Lt. Nghia's rucksack, searched by Paul Reed in March 1968.

BO QUOC PHONG
—:—

VIET NAM DAN CHU CONG HOA
Doc-Lap Tu-Do Hanh-Phuc
———————

SO : 1489 /QĐB5

BO TRUONG BO QUOC PHONG

- Can cu luat so 109/SL - L II ngay 31-5-1958
quy dinh che do phuc vu cuacy quan Quan doi nhan dan
Viet Nam .
- Can cu nghi dinh so 306/TTG ngay 20-6-1958
quy dinh cap bac quan ham hien che chinh thuc
cua quan doi nhan dan Viet Nam .
- Theo de nghi cuadong chi tong tham muu truong,
chu nhiem tong cuc chinh tri .

Q U Y E T   D I N H

Dieu I : - Nay trao quan ham cap ......Thiếu úy......
chô đồng chí ......Nguyễn. van. Nghĩa.......
so hieu ......113.792... thuoc ....
.... Sư đoàn 304

Dieu 2 : - Cac dong chi tong tham muu truong, chu nhiem ton
tong cuc Chinh tri co trach nhiem thi hanh
quyet dinh nay

Ngay 25 thang 9 nam 1965

Sao y bản chính
Phó Trưởng E24.

KT . BO TRUONG BO QUOC PHONG
Thu truong
Da ky

TRUNG ĐOÀN
24

THUONG TUONG : Song Hao

Chứng Tá : Nguyễn manh Khạch

The orders which promoted Lt. Nghia to the rank of second lieutenant. These were also in the captured rucksack.

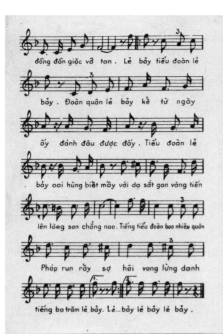

The front (top) and back (bottom) of a folded card on which a marching song was printed. This was carried by Lt. Nghia and was also in the rucksack that Paul's unit captured.

The Hien Luong Bridge (across the Ben Hai River) as it appeared in 1993. This bridge crosses the river which separated North from South. Before the arrival of American troops, NVA soldiers "infiltrated" the South by walking across this bridge. During the "American War," the bridge was closed and guarded by troops at either end who constantly played propaganda to each other over loud-speakers. The first poem in Lt. Nghia's diary was written by one of his friends, who had spent seven years as a guard at this bridge.

North Vietnamese stamps, and envelopes which were in the captured rucksack along with the diary.

(Top) a portion of the Truong Son Range (Ho Chi Minh Trail) as it now appears.
The bridge, built in 1973 by Cuban engineers, crosses the Da Krong River.
(Bottom) Paul standing beside the Thai Binh section of the Truong Son Range
cemetery near Khe Sanh.

Nguyen van
Nghia,
November 1993,
in the lobby of
the Oriental
Hotel, Da Nang.

Vu Thi Gai (Mrs. Nguyen van Nghia) on the steps of her home, November 1993.

Paul Reed's party and Nguyen van Nghia's family pose in front of Nghia's house in 1993. From the left Phil Sturholm (film crew), Dang Minh Nguyet (translator), Nghia's daughter, Nghia's son-in-law, Mrs. Nghia, Luong Thanh Nghi (translator), Nguyen van Nghia, Nghia's daughter-in-law with Nghia's new grandson, Mike James (film crew), Nghia's son, Nghia's youngest son, Paul Reed, Marc Waszkiewicz (film crew), Steve Smith (film crew).

Hostility has given way to smiles. A friendly soldier of the Peoples Army of Viet Nam sees Paul on the street and willingly poses for a photograph. He's twenty years old, not old enough to remember the war.

Nguyen van Nghia answering questions about his medals. Luong Thanh Nghi is translating.

Paul Reed and Nguyen van Nghia together in November 1993.

(Top) Paul lugs a mortar tube through the jungle near hill 1064 in March 1968. (Bottom) Twenty-five years later, Paul and Mr. Nghia walk together along a trail in the same area near hill 1064.

the opium and heroin some of the soldiers obtained in the South. Living in the safety of a secured area was depressing. He felt out of place, not waiting to kill or die.

Hawaii seemed to him more stressful than Vietnam. He was more anxious to leave the state than he had been to leave Vietnam after his first combat experience.

The return to Vietnam did not work, though. The reality of the place was also stressful. He had become comfortable with killing, but the peace of Hawaii had sensitized him to the fact that he really could die. He wanted to live and he applied for another seven days, this time in Okinawa.

For some reason the request for a week off was granted. Paul grabbed his M-16, his packed rucksack, and took the next outbound helicopter to where he could rendezvous with a Lockheed C-130 that flew him to Okinawa.

The leave was not what he thought it would be. Half glad to be getting back, he was on the way to rejoin his unit when he happened to walk past the hospital at Qui Nhon. He was surprised to hear someone shout, "Paul! Paul! Come on up. The whole platoon's up here, man." The voice was that of his closest friend, Jerry Thomas from Sheffield, Alabama. Paul assumed that "whole platoon" was an exaggeration. Even though Paul's platoon had been reduced to squad size by combat losses, there were still thirteen men in it. But to his amazement, a dozen of the men were in hospital beds. Only one member of the entire platoon was missing from the ward—Paul Reed. While he was on leave, the men had been ambushed on a search-and-destroy operation. No one escaped without serious wounds, if they lived at all. Most were missing body parts and would soon be shipped out to Japan. Paul never saw them again. He felt guilty, even though it would have made no difference at all if he had been with his buddies when the attack came. The inexorable reality of the tactical situation was such that every man would have been hit regardless of the platoon's strength. If he had been there, Paul simply would have been wounded or dead like the rest of them. But truth is no part of the mixture of guilt and imagined invincibility that are the makeup of youthful soldiers. Reed had not been maimed or

killed while on active duty in the past, so he "knew" that somehow his presence would have helped the men. It was irrational,
but so was the war.

The more Paul talked, the more he sought understanding
from men and women who had no sense of what war was all
about, the more isolated he felt. He was denounced by college
professors and students alike. Some people criticized him
because the war had not been won. Some criticized him for
being foolish enough to go. He was called a psychotic killer and
a fool, bloodthirsty, and naive. Even among members of the
Veterans of Foreign Wars, there was a distaste for those who
served in Vietnam. World War II was the last "good" war, and
Korea had at least some support. But Vietnam was fought by
killers and losers. Instead of support, Reed came to feel shame.

For a period of time, Reed was as low as he could get. Had
he not had custody of Silas, he might have chosen the alterna-
tive to life. Instead, he found himself on his hands and knees
praying, asking God for guidance. Finally, he focused on the
idea Dale Doucet had proposed. Feeling direction from God, he
decided to return Nghia's diary to his widow and children.

Steve Smith, a documentary filmmaker/photographer from
Seattle, heard about Paul Reed and wanted to record the event.
There would be great visual drama in seeing the man who may
have killed Mrs. Nghia's husband return the most intimate possession remaining. Smith made contact with the North
Vietnamese in Hanoi for permission to film the event and to
enlist their help in finding the widow and/or his children. They
were delighted and agreed to let Paul give back the diary.

It was October 29, 1993 when Steve Smith came to Dallas
to film a segment on Paul prior to his scheduled November 1
return to the land where both his friends and a portion of his
soul had died. In the midst of the interview, during which Reed
was talking about his grief over his former enemy's death, a
man he had come to know and care about through his writings,
Smith quietly said, "There's no other way to tell you this than
to just come out and tell you. Nguyen van Nghia is alive and
he's eager to meet you."

Reed looked at Smith for a moment, smiling, numb. His
words were a jumble. "Wow, man, that's incredible. He wants

to meet me? You're kidding…some heavy stuff." And then he broke. His head fell and tears began streaming down his cheeks.

The emotions were overwhelming. Nguyen van Nghia was the man Paul had once hunted in the jungles of Vietnam. He was a man he never knew during those months of active duty, yet he was a man he would have killed without hesitation.

Later, after rediscovering the box two decades after the war was over, Nguyen van Nghia had become Reed's friend and constant companion. He had placed the soldier's photograph on a corner of his computer screen. He had read and reread the translation of the diary, always finding something new in it to touch his heart. He had clung to the artifacts as a lifeline to the humanity he once thought the army and the war had destroyed. When he finally had the courage to let go, to return the items to people he knew needed them more than he did, he thought of their reactions to the man whose unit had killed many vietnamese, perhaps some of their relatives.

And now there was one less death on his conscience, one less victim of a cold-blooded teenager who had gone from killing-to-live to living-to-kill. More important, the enemy whose blood he had not shed was the enemy who had restored a piece of his soul.

Always, my love, I miss your rosy cheeks;
Your boat has docked inside me forever.
Do you remember the quiet evenings,
The sunset reflecting on the water,
The wind tossing your hair?

The breaking waves laugh in time;
Perhaps the water can measure time.
Please keep track of our memories.
We said good-bye, now we are apart.
The boat has taken my girl home.
That evening my heart writhed in pain.
I love, I suffer.
Her boat still parts the evening waters.
Darling, forget me not.

Be happy during your spring years.
Be sad no longer, lest my heart irreparably break.

Always remember our promises
To be faithful and forever in love.
Our love is truly wondrous;
Our hair will turn gray together.
You smile, your lips blossom with
Hope for tomorrow.
Today, on the border, I take in the horizon;
Believing tomorrow will come.

On November 3, 1993, a Thai Airline plane touched down at Noi Bai Airport, Hanoi, with Paul Reed onboard. It was the city of his nightmares, the capitol of the enemy territory he had once fought so fiercely. He had hated the city without ever having seen it. Now he was there and he felt the anger well up inside him once again.

There was military equipment on the ground. He spotted several Russian MIG jet fighters, a radar unit, and a building with some tall antennas he knew to be a communication center. These were primary targets, and for an instant Reed thought he had infiltrated an objective he would need to destroy.

The communication equipment was especially disconcerting. Hanoi Hannah had been the propaganda voice of the North Vietnamese radio broadcast to the Americans. She was their equivalent of Tokyo Rose—a comforting voice meant to demoralize the soldiers by talking about such matters as how they were losing the war and the way their girlfriends were cheating on them back home. Hanoi Hannah ironically used the same approach as the AIT drill instructor, creating her own version of Jody. What she did not realize was that the Americans had coupled the concept of Jody with anger towards Mr. Charles. Reed and others would listen to her, then resolve to fight harder, more viciously.

The plane rolled to the terminal. The other passengers were calm, perhaps a little curious about where they would be going, but generally not questioning what was happening. Only Paul was having a problem, and he forced himself to look out the windows, first right and then left, pretending to be a tourist, taking in his first sights of the country.

The doors opened and the other passengers disembarked. Unlike his first time when he had jammed the exit and tried to flee, Reed sat trembling on his seat. He knew who he was—Paul Reed, civilian, Dallas, Texas, long-distance trucker, father of Silas, former husband of two wives. He also worried that such an identity was only his to keep so long as he stayed on the airplane. The cabin was his link with the present. Stepping off the plane was his link to the past. It was a past he remembered with horror. It was a past to which he had returned too often in his nightmares. It was a past he wanted to bury, and he feared it was outside the door.

Finally, Reed was the only passenger left. He had to rise, had to take his hand luggage and camera, had to walk down the aisle, past the flight attendant, and down the steps pushed against the plane.

The day was hot, the sun bright, the sky clear. Despite the presence of the military equipment, there were no sounds of battle. Neither automatic weapons nor the sound of mortars could be heard. Neither cordite nor the smell of rotting flesh lingered in the wind.

Reed went through customs. The bureaucrats were young men and women who were barely out of diapers when their fathers were trying to kill Reed and his friends. If they were the faces of his former enemies, they were a generation removed. Their hearts were not filled with hate. Their hands were not stained with blood. This new generation was nature's way of cleansing the soul of the land in the same manner as when the first flowers once again burst into bloom on what had formerly been the killing fields of Vietnam.

Paul instinctively glanced at the men on duty. He saw two North Vietnamese, apparently security or officials of some sort, unarmed, smiling. They seemed happy to see him, their body posture relaxed. There were no hidden messages, no danger.

The first Vietnamese who spoke to Reed smiled, extended his hand, and introduced himself as Luong Thanh Nghi. He was twenty-nine years old, handsome, spoke excellent English, and would serve as translator. A second man, much older, was also with him. He said his name was Nguyen van Luong and he would be Reed's driver and guide. He was a war veteran himself, having been in the war against France which the Vietnamese won during the battle at Dien Bien Phu. He was proud of his service to his country, proud that he had been honored for heroism. The fact that he had a government job as a guide demonstrated that his country respected and honored him. He showed Paul a photograph of himself and a friend, both in uniform, that had been taken during their time of service.

"Have you met Mr. Nghia?" Paul asked the translator. "Does he know I'm coming? What kind of person is he? Does he want to meet me?"

Nghi smiled and said, "Yes, he knows you're coming and he's expecting you. He's an older man. A very nice gentleman."

The comment about the age startled Reed. He had assumed that he and Nghia were contemporaries. If Nghia was older, he might be in his late forties or early fifties, but Reed had the impression that wasn't what the interpreter meant by the statement he made. "Older? How much older?"

"I think he's about sixty-five," said the interpreter.

Paul was startled. The photograph he had studied obsessively was that of a much younger man. The idea that he might be a generation removed from his former enemy was not something he had anticipated. It should have made no difference, yet he was suddenly confused. He took the photograph he "knew" was that of Nghia and showed it to the interpreter. "You mean, this is not the man I'm coming to see?" he asked.

The interpreter looked at it curiously, as though wondering why Paul had it at all. "That's right," he replied. "That's not him."

The interpreter explained more of Nghia's history as he and Paul journeyed to the home of his former enemy. He had been born on August 10, 1928, to a couple who were poor peasants, and who died while he was still a boy. Instead of being doomed to the same life of grinding poverty that they had known, he was given a chance to go to school where he studied both letters (reading and writing) and what was called "the operation," the Vietnamese equivalent of addition, subtraction, multiplication, and division. It was a very simple school, somewhat similar to the American one-room schoolhouse found in rural areas. But it was enough for his intellect to be noted and for him to eventually receive training as a political instructor during what the Vietnamese called the American War.

Nghia first went into the army when he was seventeen years old—just a few months older than Paul. His parents had died fairly recently, his brothers lived apart from each other, and he had not yet met his wife. The French dominated the nation, and he traveled among all the provinces in the Northern plain in order to fight.

War terrified Nghia, but he was intensely patriotic. He related to the leaders of the past who fought generation after generation to free their land of foreign domination. He would do his best, knowing it did not matter if he lived or died, so long as he served his country well.

It was 1957 when Nghia finally was able to marry. He worked the land—a peasant faced with the same intense hard work that had led to his parents' early death. But his life was a little better and he had four children, his first son being born in 1959. When the American War was increasing in intensity, his wife and children encouraged him to again join the army. The year was 1965, he was thirty-seven years old and a veteran. Yet they all felt that he had to do something for the nation, even though it might mean never returning.

Nghia's family received a small sum of money when he returned to duty. However, though they planned to spend time together, there was never an opportunity. Sometimes the war was too intense and Nghia too far from home for him to make a visit. At other times the area set aside for rest and recreation was not safe; random American patrols created great danger for anyone passing through the area.

Nghia frequently wrote letters to his wife, but getting them to her was difficult. During the five years that he served in the South, only one of his letters made it back home.

The Nghias had a reversal of the traditional relationship because his wife had to raise crops, make money, and take care of the family in her husband's absence. The situation was not unusual in the American War, though. Many women had their husbands serving in the South. They were forced to live in the same nontraditional way as women lived in the United States during the Second World War. At that time the women went from being housewives or living with their parents to working in factories and running businesses. They developed an independence that changed their attitudes when the men returned and wanted to resume their traditional social dominance. The same occurred in North Vietnam, though in Nghia's family, he was so respected that his wife and children continued to defer to him even though he sustained such severe war wounds that he could never work the land again.

Nghia's health had been damaged severely in Kontum Province when he was helping to gather wounded soldiers from the battlefield after the Americans had retreated a few hundred yards. An American plane sprayed the area with a chemical the Vietnamese called "toxicosis." He went into shock, his body alive with pain, his eyes stinging. He could not see, and though his eyes could have been repaired in the United States, the facilities available to him could only restore limited vision.

Nghia's wife was told that he was killed in 1968. They knew when he left that he was to stay and fight for the duration of the war or until he died, so it came as a surprise when he walked the hundreds of miles back home, turning up at the house unexpectedly. His body had been severely damaged, and he sustained malaria during his walk north along the Ho Chi Minh Trail. But the most serious damage was to his eyesight, a fact that made him useless to the military despite his having been promoted to the rank of first lieutenant.

The sudden return was both joyful and sad. Nghia's wife had aged prematurely. She was thinner than he remembered, the result of limited food and intensely hard work. Her skin, her hair, her slightly stooped body were all older than her years. Yet love transcended their awareness of how much each had changed and they rejoiced in again being together. She knew he would never again be able to provide for his family, yet she and their children encouraged him to tell them how to handle the land and the money they earned. He was the honored head of the house, and so they helped him maintain his self-respect, an important issue for an older Vietnamese male and something many of his comrades in arms lost within their families.

What Paul did not realize was that Nghia did not share his
emotions about the meeting of two former enemies. Nghia followed the religious beliefs of the ancients. The past, whether the
day earlier or a lifetime ago, was over. It had no meaning. Only
the present and the future were significant. When Paul Reed was
stalking him in the jungle of Vietnam, he was the enemy, a man
to destroy. The moment Nghia left the battlefield, Reed was not
his enemy. The war ended, and with it the anger, the hatred, and
the desire for revenge. He understood that what was appropriate
in times of violence was not appropriate in time of peace. He
neither hated nor feared Paul Reed. The shooting had stopped,
and so far as he was concerned, for the twenty years since the
war had ended, the man who had once been his enemy was
already his friend.

The airport terminal had several peddlers waiting to sell their
wares. Reed remembered the vendors in South Vietnam, remembered the way every price was at least double retail so they could
either negotiate down and still make a good profit or take advantage of the foreigners. This was no exception, though Paul did not
realize it until he purchased an English/Vietnamese phrase book.
The asking price was two dollars, but he quickly learned that the
selling price had always been just one dollar. He bought it,
amused that some facts of Vietnam life had never changed.

Reed was taken to the Government Guest House in downtown Hanoi, a western-style hotel similar to what had been
found when the country was under French colonial rule. The
room was pleasant, quiet, and contained almost flawless indoor
plumbing, something of a surprise to Paul. Only the shower was
a problem because it was a hand-held nozzle that barely worked.
He had to squat in the bathtub, hold the shower nozzle with one
hand, try to cover himself with an adequate amount of water,
and scrub with the other hand.

There was a small refrigerator in the room, several bottles of
water, and glasses which appeared to be clean. There was a
French brand in clear plastic and something unfamiliar that had
been boiled and placed in a hard bottle. He settled on the one in
the clear plastic.

That night, Paul and the film crew went to the Piano
Restaurant and Bar on Hang Vai Street for dinner. Again, it was

more sophisticated than he expected. This was a country where many people, including Nghia, had no indoor plumbing. A single electric outlet was often the only inside power. They had developed the technology and many people had incomes adequate to enjoy it, but the old ways were still acceptable—plumbing and electricity were not considered essentials after thousands of years without them.

The restaurant specialized in Vietnamese and Chinese cuisines, and Reed delighted in authentic fried rice. He also wanted to take breakfast back to his room, so he ordered bananas before leaving. He thought he was speaking properly, using both his memory and the Vietnamese/English phrase book he had purchased. However, instead of what he desired, an elaborate dish of flaming brandy-soaked bananas was presented to him. It reminded Paul of a birthday party at a Red Lobster restaurant, when the waiters and waitresses bring out a cake with flaming candles. The film crew looked at each other with amazement.

It was late when the men finished their dinner, and the hotel was far enough from the restaurant that they decided to hail a cyclo-driver. This was a type of rickshaw powered by a solo driver. Competition among the men who operated them was fierce, and the effort to hail one brought fifteen drivers instantly vying for business.

The cyclo-drivers had the same reckless abandon as New York City taxi drivers. In all of Hanoi, there are only two or three intersections controlled by traffic signals. Collisions are frequent and rides can be quite wild as the drivers weave in and out, vying with each other for space on the crowded back streets of Hanoi. Only the tourists are saved from the constant jostling of vehicles coming too close together. The drivers ring a handbell every few feet to alert passersby to the fact that the passenger is a foreigner. The bell alerts the people to keep a greater distance. They want the tourists to have a more pleasant ride, apparently to assure their return. It is a little like the New York City campaign several years earlier when the taxi drivers, infamous for being surly to all and especially to those from out of town, were encouraged to be polite. Classes were held to teach them how to be friendly, and the effort was fodder for the monologues of many comedians. Apparently, Hanoi is trying something similar.

Paul felt certain he would sleep well, but by three o'clock in the morning he knew that sleep might be impossible. His eyes were open, alert for an ambush. He was not having a flashback to the jungles. He knew he was in a hotel in Hanoi. He just could not adjust to the fact that the war was over, that the tall American was no longer a target for a bullet, a grenade, or a knife. He wondered if the VC would sneak up on him.

He moved from bed quietly, the stealth of jungle warfare returning as though it had only been days since his last patrol. He checked for movement, for sound. He made his sense come alive, then crept to the door leading to the balcony of his room. It was still shut and locked, no one having tampered with it.

Slowly, he opened the door, and moved on to the balcony. He scanned the darkness, the points from which someone could move in for an attack. All was quiet, peaceful. The only stress came from the humidity that was so thick it was like being enveloped in a rain cloud about to release its moisture.

Reed stood silently in the shadows, listening for two or three minutes. There was no movement, no enemy. Still he was restless, not becoming calm for another hour. He wrote in a journal he had been maintaining, watched a lizard move up the wall, and tried to relax. Eventually, exhaustion took over and he slept for a couple of hours, awakening to the soft sound of chimes.

Reed ran to the window, checking the clock as he went. It was 6:00 A.M., daylight was just beginning, and already people were awake. He saw an aggressive game of badminton being played, and street noises indicated that people were going to and from work. He, too, wanted to be up, and since he could not eat in his room as planned, he went out for bananas, papaya, orange juice, and buttered toast. Then he joined the translator, the guide, and four members of the documentary production crew who would be filming his meeting with Nghia, a man they had already met.

The trip to Thai Binh City, capital of Thai Binh Province where Nghia lived, took three and a half hours. The road was jammed with bicycles and motorcycles, slowing their journey to a maximum of thirty miles an hour. Frequently, the driver leaned on his horn to alert people that the large vehicle would be passing. Again, nothing was what Reed expected, including the friendly people who smiled and waved, unconcerned by the foreigner in their midst.

Once in Thai Binh City, Mr. Nghi said it would be polite to take certain members of the Province People's Committee, including the foreign relations expert, Miss Dang Minh Nguyet, a committeewoman fluent in English; Pham Quang Khanh, Vice-Chairman of the People's Committee; and Bui Manh Hung, a police officer. They were the ones who had helped track down Nghia and his family for the documentary photographer, and they were anxious to see the meeting of the two men.

Reed noticed another unexpected reaction. The van held nine passengers, and with the additions there were ten in all. No problem, this was Vietnam. Besides, Miss Nguyet was an extremely beautiful young woman, highly intelligent and very friendly. Even though her clothing was conservative, Reed could see that she had an attractive figure. When it came time to board the van and leave, he positioned himself so that she had to sit wedged close to him during the overcrowded ride to Nghia's home. The other passengers looked at him with knowing disapproval. Never mind, there was a sense of chemistry that delighted him. He saw her as a woman, and realized that she was not a gook. He realized that for the first time he was seeing her as he would any woman, and he knew that more healing was taking place.

Reed was scared as he approached Nghia's home. It was in what looked like an alleyway with two-story buildings on their right and one-story buildings on the left. The right side was for commerce, the lower floor used for whatever business the owner was in, and the upper floor reserved for living quarters.

The street-alley was just wide enough for a van. Tall vegetation obscured the view down a smaller pathway, just off the wider street, where the interpreter told the driver to stop. The foliage reminded Reed of areas where he and the other men used to set up ambushes during the war. His training told him to never use a trail. The reality of this trip indicated he had to do so, even if a sniper's bullet awaited him.

"Are you ready?" asked the interpreter.

Paul Reed did not know. Several children had gathered and were silently staring at him. He wondered if he was really that different. He wondered if they had ever seen an American. He wondered if he should turn and run, look for a weapon, refuse to go on.

Before he and Mr. Nghi, the interpreter, went those last several steps, Paul looked at the interpreter and asked if he would introduce him. He was visibly frightened, a small boy reaching desperately for an adult's hand to give him comfort in a scary encounter. His face seemed younger, and his body seemed to grow pale. He thought of asking if Nghia had any AK-47s or grenades, but fortunately decided not too out of respect.

The men rounded the corner, the interpreter introducing them. Mr. Nghia was in front, dressed in a green shirt and slightly darker green pants, his family lined up close to the house, watching, their expressions noncommittal. Reed and Nghia looked into each other's eyes, the American seeing only gentleness and a degree of nervousness. *This is the guy who writes poetry?* thought Reed, reaching out his hand.

Nghia took both of Reed's hands in his own. The American was much larger, his hands capable of engulfing those of Nghia. But Nghia held them the way a father might hold those of a child sitting up in bed, afraid of whatever lurks in the darkness. The older man was at once loving and reassuring, saying more with a touch and a look than Reed could express in words. Yet Reed realized that Nghia's knees were shaking slightly. Reed wasn't without nervousness himself and mistakenly addressed Mr. Nghia with the interpreter's similar name.

"I'm very pleased to meet you, Mr. Nghi," said Reed. The interpreter ignored the mistake and translated. "How do you do?" Paul had been thinking about what he would say ever since he knew Nghia was alive. Nothing seemed quite right, so in the end he settled for something innocuous.

"I'm fine, thank you. Won't you join me for tea?" Then he took Reed by the hand and led him into the house. The front doors and windows were wide open as they usually were in North Vietnam. The openness was somehow comforting.

Nghia was as nervous as Reed. The invitation to tea was customary, a ritual of politeness. And when they entered the home, small by American standards but quite comfortable for the Vietnamese, there were several people sitting on a rice mat bed at one end of the room. Paul did not know if they were family members, neighbors, or someone else who came to see the American. Certainly, there was more company than normal, for every place to sit was taken—small chairs, the windowsill, even each other's laps. All were smiling. All seemed genuinely glad to see Reed.

At the other end of the room were a table and eight chairs. Eight teacups on eight saucers had been arranged around the table. The very best china was being used.

Still frightened of the unknown, Paul hoped to sit on the chair placed closest to the door. He wanted to be able to flee, to leave the house, leave the country. Nghia would have nothing to do with his wishes, though. It was important that he show deference for his wife—the woman he loved, the one to whom so much of his writing was dedicated—and the son, who let him retain his pride by using him as an "advisor" after he returned shattered by the war. Nghia would sit on their guest's left, his wife on the right. He was honoring her, and Reed's fears would have to be ignored in favor of honoring his wife.

The conversation briefly turned to Reed's family. Again, a ritual. He was then supposed to ask about Mr. Nghia's. But Paul, although warned of this ritual, forgot it when he arrived. He failed to ask Nghia about his own family, but the Vietnamese ignored the mistake. Such manners seemed of minor consequence given the importance of the moment.

The men sat together, hands folded in their respective laps, their bodies tense. There was no anger, no hint of hostility. Rather, it was the nervousness of a blind date, of courtship without knowledge of the other person. Finally, Nghia tried to become more personal.

"I am very moved and very pleased to have you here in my home," said Nghia. "It is quite a long trip to Vietnam. You got my pack during the war. Now you bring it to my home. I am so very happy."

Reed explained that he did not bring the full pack. He only had a few things, but they were ones he knew would be important to Nghia.

As Paul spoke, hesitantly at first, then more comfortable about telling the story of mailing the diary home where it sat on a shelf for more than twenty years, he glanced at Nghia's wife. She was seated on his right, acting as though they were long-time friends. She made Paul feel at home, having none of the hesitancy, nervousness, or reservations apparent in her husband. Yet she was the one to whom Paul thought he would be delivering the diary. He had until only recently believed that she was a widow, the one who had suffered for Paul's actions, the one to whom he could never make amends. He had thought himself the soldier who had robbed her of a husband and father to their children. Now he knew that his fantasy had never been true. His enemy had been alive, though physically hurt and emotionally at least as shattered as himself. Yet that pain was the price of war for every man. What mattered to Paul was that this was one North Vietnamese soldier who had lived, not died at Paul's hands.

Doesn't she know who she's sitting next to? Reed wondered to himself. He marveled at her appearance. She was dressed in the customary black pants, though with a pink button-down, long-sleeve blouse. Her hair was pulled back in a bun wrapped in a brown piece of cloth. She was smaller than her husband, very feminine, with a smile so rich and radiant, it seemed to emanate from her heart. Her face was lined from the stress of the years, yet there was a happiness there, as though the work was a necessity and not something she ever begrudged.

Hasn't he told her I was the enemy who tried to kill her husband during the war? he wondered. And then he realized the type of woman she was. As with her husband, the past is always over and must not color the present. Had he killed her husband during the war, the act of returning the diary would have resulted in the same warm, friendly greeting. She was as sensitive to life as her poet/soldier husband. The hate-filled anger that had so thoroughly consumed Reed during the last decades was not comprehensible to the couple. Just as the war had to be fought as savagely as necessary to win, so the peace had to be lived with enduring gentleness, love, and respect for the former enemy.

Nghia's daughter and two of his three sons, along with a daughter-in-law, son-in-law, and grandchild, were there. The other people were friends. It was an important time for them, a chance to meet an American who had faced their father during one of Vietnam's many wars. They knew who Paul Reed was, what he had done. But they cared about the Paul Reed of today. They were delighted to meet him, to enjoy his company. He was the first American ever to visit their village.

The atmosphere was like being newly married and having dinner at an in-law's house where everyone knows you, likes you, and wants you to be comfortable. Mrs. Nghia poured the tea, and Paul practiced his limited knowledge of the Vietnamese language.

Reed was shocked. He was having tea with a former NVA. He had hated this man, hated his family, his beliefs, everything about him. Yet he liked him, realized that he respected him more than he did many Americans who had failed to do their duty—most notably, one who claims he never inhaled. Nghia had made a stand and fought for what he believed was right. He did not run. It was something Paul could understand.

The talk and the ritual of the tea continued. Then, before it was time to exchange the old possessions, there was one last rite to perform. Nghia brought out his finest rice liquor.

Paul did not drink liquor. He had gone through many traumas in his life and had found that liquor was one more escape from reality. Yet he knew it would be an insult to not participate.

Nghia filled their tea cups, then the two toasted each other. Pretending to savor the moment, Reed sniffed the liquid, realized it was strong, wondered what to do as he noticed Nghia taking the cup and drinking it all. Then, with a hesitant smile, he looked at Reed. There was no further delay.

Reed lifted the cup to his mouth and swallowed. The liquid was like a fire slipping down his throat, singeing his nose, the roof of his mouth, his tonsils. He felt his stomach come alive with heat, as though he had been filled with glowing coals. Unable to help himself, he coughed twice, then awkwardly smiled and managed to croak, "Excellent." He looked to the side to hide his watering eyes. He hoped that if anyone noticed the tears, they would think the emotions were for the meeting, not because the liquor was so potent.

Reed told of reading the diary, of coming to realize that he and Nghia were the same. They were two men doing their duty as they understood it, following what they believed in. He explained how touched he was by the writing of his wife. He said that in the diary, Nghia commented that the sons looked like him, his daughter like his wife. Seeing them in the home, he realized that Nghia had been right, a statement that delighted the family.

Reed asked Nghia what he remembered about the war. Very little, Nghia explained. The bombing by the B-52s had affected his memory. His left eye was blinded in the war. His right eye saw little.

Finally, Reed pulled the possessions from an envelope he carried. There was a reluctance on his part. For twenty-five years, the contents of the pack had been his own. More recently, when the items were rediscovered, they had become talismans, magic charms to help him heal. He was as intimately attached to them as Nghia must have been when living and fighting in South Vietnam. Yet they were captured possessions, not rightfully his own. He had to give them back, even though in doing so, he realized he was losing what had been a crutch—something to help him in the transition from hate to healing. It was a difficult moment and he brought out the least important items first.

"This is my scissors," Nghia explained upon receiving the first item. "We would use it to cut each other's hair."

The stamps were next. Nghia said that in the five years of fighting, only one of his letters ever made it home.

For the first time the diary took on an additional importance. One letter in five years to the woman who was raising his four children. She believed in Nghia's love, was faithful to him, undoubtedly had talked intimately for many hours after his return. But the diary would be proof that he had not forgotten her, not forgotten the children, cherished them all. It would reinforce his feelings and thinking during that time apart in a way nothing else could do.

The pictures came next, all slightly embarrassing for Nghia but delighting his children and friends. There was a custom among friends to exchange small photographs when leaving. Reed noted one particularly beautiful young woman who Nghia said was the sister of his friend. It was the only time Mrs. Nghia seemed slightly angry. She looked at the image with tight lips and fire in her eyes. Whatever happened so very long ago was not something she wanted her husband to remember.

The pictures of other pretty girls brought laughter to his children at his obvious discomfort. Nghia tried to explain that pretty girls often gave passing soldiers their photographs. He was as embarrassed as if the girls were still young like their images, not old and probably grandparents like himself. He obviously had made peace with his enemy but not with the flirtations enjoyed by a lonely soldier meeting a friendly face while trying to survive in enemy territory.

Reed was beginning to like Nghia too much. In his heart, he knew where he was, what was taking place. But in his anguished thoughts was the idea that this might not be the right man. They might have brought him to some other Nguyen van Nghia. They might want to deceive him, perhaps to hurt him. He did not know what was taking place, and the lack of control scared him.

He showed him a picture inscribed "Your loving sister," and Nghia could not identify the face. Reed was angry, suddenly certain he had been shown to the wrong man, the wrong family.

"That's my southern sister," Nghia finally explained, as though that would clarify everything. What Reed did not understand was the use of the word "southern sister" in the Vietnamese language and culture. A supportive friend who believed in the same politics, in the goals of the war for unification, would have received this title. This had nothing to do with an intimate relationship, and the meeting together might have been brief, perhaps only a few moments, the pictures exchanged as proof of support.

Yet Reed was becoming uneasy. His paranoia was returning and he began to seriously wonder if he was with the correct Nguyen van Nghia. He wondered if the government had made a switch. This was a different man with the same name. This was ...

Then he remembered the identification card with the picture taken when Nghia was young. The description told of a number of identifying marks, including a small black scar under the right side of his chin. He brought it out and mentioned the scar, at which a delighted Dien, one of Nghia's sons, jumped up, came to his father, and pointed to the scar underneath his chin, the one on the ID card. Reed smiled and thought, "This is my man. He's the right Nguyen van Nghia." There was no longer any question.

Later, when Reed was calmer, he realized that he had fed his own suspicions by being unrealistic. The war was not indelibly etched in Reed's memory. That was not the reason he could remember details of the battles in Kontum Province that Nghia could not. The nature of the United States was such that everyone, soldiers and civilians alike, had access to what were called military "after action" reports. In fact, shortly before he made the trip, three of his friends, Lewis ("Stony") Stoneking, Bill ("Billy Joe") Jang, and former platoon leader John B. Doan had sent him letters reminding him of the details.

The photograph Reed thought was Nghia turned out to be a Vietnamese friend who was later killed in the war. The interpreter at the airport had been correct about the mistake Reed had made.

At last, there was the diary. As Reed reached into the envelope, he silently prayed, "God, give me the forgiveness I need for this man, and repair my heart." Then he spoke aloud, saying: "This small book helped me see you as a good person. Before I read the small book…" His eyes began filling with tears. His face was strained. He spoke slowly, determined that the interpreter would hear and understand all his words so that Nghia would know what was in his heart. "I did not like you. You and your unit killed some of my friends."

Nghia looked into the American's face. His was also filled with emotion. There was no anger, no shame. He was facing the reality of war that all soldiers must face. There are two sides filled with patriots, friends, men and women with loved ones and families. Each thinks they are right, the other wrong. And each causes what can be unspeakable anguish in the name of honor, duty, country. As Reed spoke, he was becoming aware of this reality, something Nghia seemed to have understood long before the American arrived.

"And I want you to know that I hated you very severely. But you lost friends, too. And you said in your small book here that you were angry at me, too."

Nghia nodded, smiling.

"Are you still angry?"

Reed began to relax. The emotions of the moment had overwhelmed him, but he finally realized he needed to heal. They were no longer men at war against each other. They were comrades in arms who had worn different uniforms, come from different locations, fought for different sides only because of an accident of birth.

"Forget the past," said Nghia, both he and Reed smiling. "Now we are friends. I'm grateful it's past. I'm very happy that I lived to see this day." He took the American's hand in his.

"Do you forgive me and my unit?" asked Reed.

It was a question Paul Reed had not expected to ask. From the moment he realized he would be seeing his old enemy and not the man's widow, Paul Reed had retained the emotional blinders of the previous two decades. He had failed to see that there were three sides to the conflict instead of two. He refused to think about the civilians who had been maimed by napalm, the liquid fire that adhered to human flesh and could cause severe scarring with even a mild exposure. He refused to think about the people who had lost loved ones, homes, and a way to earn a living. He refused to think that the men of North Vietnam paid a much higher price during the war than the men of the United States, most of whom were rotated out after a single year of active combat duty.

And he refused to see that when two parties are in conflict, there is each person's side, and there is a truth which often lies somewhere in the middle of the two.

Reed looked into Nghia's eyes, his emotions again intensely visible on his face. His trip had been fueled by a mix of anger and curiosity, of the need to heal and the perceived need to confront. Nghia was the focus for the demons that still haunted his nights, his flashbacks, his work, and his intimate relationships. And now he realized that he had been wrong in part, that each had similar feelings for the other for similar reasons. And of the two, the older man had come to such understanding first.

"Yes," Nghia said quickly. He understood.

Unexpectedly, the men embraced. It was an uncomfortable moment for the friends and family members. They shifted in their seats, looking at each other, not understanding. They had not been soldiers. They had not been enemies. Many had not been alive until after both the American War and the civil war were over. They had only known a unified Vietnam, the war visible primarily through the scarred bodies and minds of the survivors. But Paul Reed wept in the arms of the only man who could understand the emotions of that instant. And so they were oblivious to the others, smiling as they separated.

Two enemies.

Two friends.

9

CHAPTER NINE

The importance of the diary had not been understood by Reed. Although some of its contents were intensely personal, most of it was intended to be shared with Nghia's fellow soldiers. Lieutenant Nghia was his unit's party officer. His role was not that of KGB-like political enforcer that Americans might imagine on the basis of our Hollywood educations. Rather, his job was closer to what we would call a morale officer. He was older than his comrades and was viewed by them much like an uncle. They would come to him with problems. At other times, he would encourage them. He found that reading inspiring poetry aloud was something that his charges really appreciated. So he recorded not only some of his own poetry, but also some poems of others that he found uplifting. The poetry in his book had been as special to the men of his unit as it had come to be to Paul. It expressed what was in all their hearts, and each time Nghia read the work to the others, often in the darkest moments between battles, his friends were deeply moved. They felt that nothing else so perfectly reflected their own feelings of why they were spending what might be the rest of their lives in the jungles of the South.

Lieutenant Nghia's "diary" was extremely important to the men of his unit because they felt that it might be the only way that the sacrifice of the average soldier could be understood by the people at home who had never been in the war. They each took a vow that if Nghia was killed, one of them would carry the diary until the war ended or it could otherwise be returned to the North. If that man was killed, another man would take possession of the cherished book. Then, ultimately, whoever was left alive would return the poetry to Thai Binh. They wanted the writing to be available within the village to serve as a memorial of the sacrifices so many of them had made. To have the poetry, along with the rest of the writing the diary contained, returned by an American was a tribute to them all.

The next item that Reed pulled from the envelope was a Viet Cong flag that Nghia had carried, though to the men of the North, it was known as the Southern Liberation flag. It had been many years since Nghia had seen such a flag. The flag had been used only in the South, and while possession of one is still legal today, displaying it on a flag pole is not. Trying to explain to Reed what it meant to him, Nghia draped it over his arm and excitedly described the symbolism of the design.

There was red on top, blue on the bottom, and a bright yellow star in the middle. The red color stood for a formerly unified country, and the yellow star stood for all the "bright, shining people." In Vietnam, blue is a color which signifies a sad spirit, so the blue on the bottom was used to represent the separated country.

Finally, all the items that Paul had taken as spoils of war were returned. "Everything you brought back means so much. But of all these things, the diary means the most. We receive a diary when we are young and keep it all our lives. I remember the day when I realized you had captured our camp. I was very sad. I thought my diary was gone forever. Now I am deeply moved that you would do this for me. Deeply moved."

Paul Reed had never thought beyond the return of Nghia's possessions. To his amazement, the joy of the moment was overwhelming for him, as though a cancerous sore had been successfully removed from a now-healing heart. He did not realize how honored he would be, and soon Mrs. Nghia invited him to stay for lunch.

The invitation was not without great consideration. Had the family not liked him, they would have remained silent. He would never know their feelings. He would have accepted that he had done what he needed to do and now the family needed to be alone. The lunch was unexpected and unwanted.

Many cultures have food that contains bacteria, viruses, and/or other problems to which immunity is developed early in life when babies are fed small amounts of the cooking. An outsider, any outsider, lacks the resistance and can become quite ill, something that had happened to Reed the one other time he dined in a Vietnamese home. He wanted to be polite, but was afraid to eat.

Nervously, Reed tried to explain this to his host and hostess. He thought that if he told them the truth, it would be better than if he tried to avoid eating, insulting them.

Mrs. Nghia laughed when he spoke of the sensitive stomachs of Americans. She said nothing about his comment, though, continuing to fix the meal while the men talked. The feast would contain enough fruit and other items that the Nghias could be honored while Paul saved face.

What was more important was the conversation that followed. The embrace, the tears, the understanding that had passed between the two men led Paul to become more candid. He wanted to know what happened to Nghia, how he lost the sight in one eye and was partially blinded in the other. He had to understand how the ravages of war had affected the man he once tried to destroy.

American infantry units, such as Paul's, used a white smoke screen created by special artillery shells or hand-thrown smoke grenades to obscure a battlefield just before an attack. This would let the American soldiers move around with less risk of being hit by aimed fire.

Some North Vietnamese apparently believed that this smoke was dropped from airplanes. At any rate, they found that rather than panicking from the sudden white-out or retreating from where they were, they could also use the smoke screen to their advantage. They could stay in place or go on the offensive at the same time as the Americans. The white cloud was a signal of tactics, not a risk in itself.

Then one day a plane swooped low over Nghia's unit, releasing a mist that looked the same to them as the white smoke, but was very different. (It was most certainly a defoliant.) Nghia and the others reacted the same as they would in response to the pre-attack smoke screens and used no protective measures.

This proved to be a terrible miscalculation. The defoliant was sprayed in order to eliminate hiding places, food, and ambush sites—in other words, to take away the tactical advantages that the jungle gave to the North Vietnamese. However, it was very toxic and could cause serious damage to sensitive areas on unprotected humans.

Nghia glanced up at the sky when he realized that something different was happening. His eyes were instantly filled with the chemical. He was blinded, and his eyes burned with pain. There was no escape because he had no idea where to go to safety.

Fortunately, one of his men took Nghia's hand and led him to their underground jungle hospital.

The doctors did the best they could, stopping the destructive effects of the chemical. Part of the damage was irreversible. Part of the damage stopped when they were able to neutralize the effects of the chemical.

For several days Nghia was in the hospital undergoing treatment. Then, when he was well, his superiors analyzed his abilities. He had limited vision, but he could still see out of one eye. He could still lead the men. His knowledge of the battlefields would still be of value. He was ordered to return to active duty, an order he expected because of the sense of duty all the men had towards their country.

It was after the return to his unit that Nghia and Reed first encountered each other without realizing it. North Vietnamese intelligence was excellent. They knew the different units, different tactics. Although Nghia's unit first thought it was the American First Cavalry Division attacking them, they quickly realized they were facing the 173rd Airborne. With a mix of pride, shame, and embarrassment, Reed asked what it was like to be on the receiving end of their assault.

"It was the roughest fighting we were ever involved in," Nghia said quietly. Then he calmly told Reed that his younger brother was killed in that battle.

Paul flashed back to what they had used in the attack. There had been endless air strikes with carpet bombing and other tactics meant to annihilate every living being. There had been artillery bombardments. They had set the land aflame with napalm.

Reed remembered the excitement of the battle, the thrill of knowing how much harm they were inflicting on the enemy. The explosions had muffled the screams, but he had fantasized the agony the enemy endured before being destroyed. What he had not known, could not have known, was that some of those screams belonged to the brother of the man in whose home he was sitting.

No one deserved what the 173rd Airborne had done that day. The attack had been a part of war, and perhaps no one deserves to have to endure war.

"Do you hate Americans?" Reed asked Nghia. He wanted them to be alike. He wanted them to hate the Americans the way the Americans hated the North Vietnamese. It wouldn't bring back Nghia's brother. It wouldn't make the war more humane. But it would bring some comfort to Reed who was trying to deal with so many feelings without success.

"No," said Nghia, he didn't hate. None of them did. "We have always admired and looked up to the Americans."

But the nicknames. Weren't there Vietnamese equivalents to "Luke the gook" or "zipperhead" used to describe the Americans?

Nghia had trouble understanding the type of bigotry Reed was describing. It was not part of their culture. It was not part of their war. They were serving in the South because they ". . . were there doing what we felt we had to do."

War was business. It was not personal. Soldiers were there to fight other soldiers. It was not part of an ideal world but it was necessary to assure unification. The concept did not weaken them as fighting men. It strengthened them as human beings.

Nghia told about the three from the village who joined the army together in 1965. Nghia and his friend Le Thang had both fought the French from 1952-1956. They had worked the fields together. They had worked in construction. They were patriots whose families encouraged them to return to uniform when the American involvement was stopping the unification of the country. Only Nghia's younger brother was serving for the first time, perhaps the reason he died while the others lived. He had less experience surviving in the midst of the violence.

Le Thang's expertise was in ambushes, and he trained the North Vietnamese fighters in this tactic. He and Nghia, each serving in different units, had been fighting the Americans from the same hill. There came a time when Le Thang had to take his men through an open area just as the Americans passed over with napalm. Le Thang became a living torch in the midst of that open area. The flesh twisted and melted like a slab of beef tossed onto a too-hot fire. His face and arms were disfigured. His legs lost so much skin that he appeared to have only charred bone to support himself. He lived, but he lived looking like some creature from a horror movie. And still Nghia did not hate, knowing that Paul's unit was the cause of his friend's anguish.

Reed's thoughts then drifted to the horrors the North Vietnamese had caused the Americans. He remembered a friend called "Sugar Bear," a marine point man who tripped a booby trap and lost both legs before being shipped home. He, too, had lived. And though he was not so disfigured as Le Thang must have been, the fact that both men could be so horribly hurt was a reminder of the brutality of war.

This time Reed fought back the tears. The enemies should have been friends. As they hurt each other, they were hurting themselves. Victory was in the eye of the beholder, neither side more deserving than the other.

It was enough talk for both men. They sat together for lunch, Mrs. Nghia providing a plate of bananas for Reed, a food he loved and which would cause him no problems. There was also some canned pork, a problem for Reed, though Nghia took his chopsticks and placed the first piece on the American's plate as a sign of respect.

Reed had not been provided with chopsticks since he was not expected to eat the rest of the food. However, when he realized that the ritual of serving was important, he used his limited knowledge of Vietnamese to say, "Mrs. Nghia, *mot doi dua, cam on yeu.*" He had meant to politely ask her to please give him some chopsticks, and noted that she seemed delighted by his efforts to use her language. He later discovered that he had unintentionally used a very personal word for "lover," but Mrs. Nghia's graciousness would not permit that her guest be embarassed. Paul practiced with the chopsticks for a moment, getting the right finger placement and balance before attempting to place some meat in Mrs. Nghia's bowl. It took him several tries, but the family appreciated the gesture.

And then it was time to leave. There was a three-and-a-half-hour drive to return to Hanoi, and he would be visiting with the Nghias again the next day.

10

CHAPTER TEN

As Paul Reed returned to Hanoi, he began to realize what war was all about. Hanoi could have been Tokyo or Berlin, Rome or Cairo, London or Moscow, Paris, Washington, DC, or even Richmond, Virginia, the capital of the Confederacy during the United States Civil War. It was the city of the designated enemy, one focus for the hatred the soldiers of the opposing army were encouraged to have as they went into battle. Hanoi had Ho Chi Minh, the leader of the gooks. Tokyo was the headquarters for the "slant-eyed yellow bellies." Berlin had the "krauts." Whatever the term that was used to keep the soldiers from focusing on the essential humanity of their enemy, there was a headquarters city on which to center their anger.

Soldiers fight more readily if they do not see their enemies as being like themselves. The decision to use the most terrible of weapons against men, women, and children—whether boiling oil and the catapult, or bombs and napalm—is made easier by an attitude that does not permit the acceptance of the enemy as a fellow human being.

To see the war through the eyes of the man he once wanted to kill, who once added to his incentive to survive battle after battle in order to destroy, caused Paul to think quite differently about life.

For years after the war, a number of Vietnam veterans complained that they never received a victory parade like the soldiers of other wars. They were unappreciated, and that was the cause of their problems.

Paul Reed knew better. He had met enough veterans of World War II, a time of celebrated victory, to know that the parade was meaningless. Patriotism and selfless sacrifice to fulfill the wishes of a nation's leaders can result in a man or woman taking actions in uniform that are against almost everything else they have been taught was right.

Paul Reed had been a Christian since he was thirteen. He was a regular churchgoer and had occasionally helped his chaplain during the time in Vietnam. He knew that the Old Testament was filled with stories of wars by and against those who considered themselves to be God's chosen people. He knew the Ten Commandments with the warning to not kill, but he also knew that when Jesus was in the midst of a city under Roman military occupation, he never condemned the soldier's life or orders. In fact, he gave tacit support to the idea of such service when he said to "render unto Caesar what is Caesar's."

He remembered the last day he was working for the modern-day rulers—the president and Congress. He was in an intense firefight, bullets, bombs, and grenades exploding everywhere. There was a chance to get on a helicopter, so his commanding officer made certain he was on it. No one wanted to think that a man minutes from having finished his tour of duty would die because he had to stay longer than necessary. His departure would not endanger anyone in his unit, just as the departure of other soldiers under similar circumstances had not hurt their comrades.

It took thirty-six hours to go from what passed as the front line in Vietnam to a relaxed seat in front of a fireplace. He had earned several medals, including the Purple Heart, but there was nothing more said to him. One minute he was in battle. A few minutes later, he was on a plane flying away from the striking range of the weapons below. And a day and a half later he was safe at home.

None of the officers for whom he had wholeheartedly served told him he had done a good job. No one thanked him for going to a strange country, then risking his life for people who were different in outward appearance, different in culture and language. One moment he was in, the next moment he was out. There was no way to discuss what he had seen and done in the context of war. There was no way to regain his perspective after months of dehumanizing the enemy in order to prepare him to fight and kill.

In hindsight he realized that he had not needed a parade. He had needed to talk, to reconcile the actions of all men in war with the expectations of men in peace. The issue was not Vietnam or Korea or Germany or Japan or England or any other nation we had fought as a people. What is proper for a civilian will result in the death of a soldier. And what is proper for a soldier on the battlefield would horrify a civilian.

Even the dehumanizing of the enemy is a tactic that can be far broader than when one country attacks another. Everyone endures mini-wars every day. The enemy might be one's boss, one's spouse, or a best friend. The dehumanizing might come through hostility that leads to the use of nicknames which can be endearing or vicious, but always are different from the name provided at birth. Sometimes these are pet names used in a more loving manner when not in the midst of an argument— "Old Man," "Old Lady," "The Boss," "The Old Goat," "the S.O.B.," etc. Other times they are harsh words under the best of circumstances, such as "bitch" or one of the terms that reduce a man or woman to the level of their body parts or an abnormal sexual act. You can't strike Shirley, the woman with whom you first made love, but you can strike the "bitch old lady" who's always on your case.

It is only when the enemy or the object of your wrath is again humanized that you can talk, can love, can develop compassion and a better way to settle differences. The army might be said to be nothing more than a reflection of society at its worst, yet filled with young idealists acting out of love for country and trust in leaders who might not have the nation's best interests at heart.

At eighteen, these were all concepts Paul could not grasp. At twenty, they were made harder because of the year in hell in the jungles of a foreign land.

Some men returned home with neither thanks from their leaders in the field nor counseling to help put what they had done in the battlefield into historical, religious, and personal perspective, and became alcoholics or drug addicts. Some turned to crime, acting out their frustrations in violence. Some entered law enforcement or fire fighting in order to use their skills, help others, and try to forget the deadly side of themselves they had not learned is in everyone.

Paul Reed eventually turned to long-distance trucking. He traveled alone for sixteen years, seeing small towns and big cities, at least from the vantage point of an eighteen-wheeler's cab, the interstate highway system, and the truck-stop diners and motels. His routes should have been partnered, though Paul insisted on driving solo. He never broke the rules, never drove dangerously long or fast, never used drugs to stay awake. He just drove to exorcise some of his demons and contain others. He could think or not, focus on the road to avoid mentally returning to the battlefield, or live out past horrors without anyone seeing him sweat, without anyone hearing him scream. But he was running away as much as if he were drinking too much or adjusting his mood through stimulants and depressants.

He did not deal with things as he had thought, of course. Two marriages and two divorces, fights picked on the highway just because he wanted to vent anger, and other actions all were increasingly irrational. Although he had been a top moneymaker for both himself and the company for which he drove, Reed lost his job, his dream home, his cherished possessions. He became so depressed he would not sleep more than three or four hours at a time. He begged twenty dollars a week from his father just so he could go out to a restaurant and order a cup of coffee whenever he pleased.

And it was all because he had never been helped to understand that the enemy was human, the enemy was in himself. He had never been told how the young can be brainwashed into converting their patriotism into unquestioning loyalty to whatever the government leaders ordered them to do. He never understood that if there was a time to fight, there was a time to heal, to neutralize the hate with love in order to get on with his life.

Until that day with Nghia.

And now he was in Hanoi, a city he once wanted to wipe off the face of the earth. Where once he would have seen gooks on the street, suddenly he was seeing men and women, infants, toddlers, and growing children. Their faces were different. Some of their mannerisms were different. Yet he had come to understand that in their hearts, they were mirrors of his own life, loves, and hopes for the future. They wanted peace, not war. They wanted to live without killing. Yet they were patriots who would travel wherever their leaders told them to go, do whatever seemed necessary to do. They were patriots just like him.

As Paul walked the streets of Hanoi on his way to Le Beaulieu Restaurant in the newly renovated Metropole Hotel, he saw both the shame and the glory of the city. There were beggars, though far fewer than the homeless seen daily on the streets of almost every major and mid-size city in the United States. One was so aggressive that he would stand outside the gate of Reed's hotel, obnoxiously getting too close, making too many demands from the "rich" foreigner. Yet Vietnam was not the United States. The beggar was wrong in his actions, wrong to so intensely pursue the American. And so Reed answered as he might have done in America. He yelled at the man to leave him alone, shouting an endless stream of insults in English. Although the people around him did not understand the words, they did understand the anger, the yelling, and were shocked by it. Screaming under any circumstance is very insulting to the Vietnamese. The beggar reacted immediately, running off and screaming his own obscenities at Paul, a few in English.

Embarrassed by his own actions, he realized he was reacting to the tension of the last few days and the contrast between his hate and the peace he was witnessing. There was great beauty in Hanoi, a city with many lakes located on the banks of the Red River. One near his hotel was called Hoan Kiem, and in the midst of the lake was a small islet on which sat a tortoise pagoda. He was told by his translator that Hoan Kiem means Lake of the Restored Sword, a name that came from the fifteenth-century legend surrounding the rule of Emperor Le Thai To. The emperor had been given a magical sword by a giant turtle, and it was to commemorate this event that the pagoda and waterway had been named.

Even the restaurant where he ate that night was different from what he expected. It was the same Metropole Hotel where Ho Chi Minh undoubtedly dined during the "American War." The hotel had been controlled and run by the French during their occupation of Indochina. After they were defeated and unification finally came to Vietnam, the French were again in charge, this time leasing the space from the Vietnamese.

It was all strange, all unexpected. The hate that had once fueled him was dissipated in the light of reality. The understanding he was developing had not yet become comfortable. He was no longer on the alert against the enemy. He was no longer convinced that death was lurking in the shadows, waiting to strike when he let himself relax. Yet there was a different type of death taking place inside him, and it caused him far greater pain.

There was nothing that could have prepared him for the feelings he experienced that day with Nghia. The adrenaline rushes, the tears, the tension and release all had taken their toll. His body felt as drained as it once had when he had to climb a steep mountainside while wearing an eighty-pound rucksack in 115-degree heat with humidity so intense he felt as though he was trying to breathe underwater.

He had survived with the fuel from the anger. Now he felt a part of him was dying—the angry part—and he feared that he could not survive without it. Not here, anyway. Not in the land of his enemy/friend. He wanted to flee the country, go home. The change was happening too fast, too out of control.

There were only five thousand people living in Nghia's village, and Nghia knew most of them. Many had never seen an American. Many knew of the American War only from their parents and teachers. Their lives had been ones of peace, the losses that devastated their families a part of their history, not of their direct knowledge. They were curious about this tall man who had come so far, and many were waiting to see him.

Reed lined up the people who had come to see him, then took their picture. They were all smiling, happy, delighted by the unusual experience.

It was time to again go into Nghia's home, but before he did, Paul stood by the van, once more attempting to prepare his emotions. An older man came up to him, filled with curiosity, oblivious to the turmoil in the American's mind. He had not fought in either the American War or the war in the South, as the civil war was known to him, but he had heard many stories about the excellent fighting ability of the Vietnamese soldiers. He asked about Reed's opinion of them, a question similar to one Reed had asked of Nghia the previous day, though then he had been talking about his airborne unit.

Reed said that the Vietnamese soldiers he had encountered were often brave and good fighters, even when facing insurmountable odds and overwhelming air and artillery support. That knowledge, that the men were good soldiers, seemed to please him. He then said he wanted to share a poem with Reed that Ho Chi Minh taught everyone from the North. It was one that he and everyone else of his generation had committed to memory when it was written in 1968, and he sang the words as his translator repeated them in English.

Last year we gained great victory
This year we would gain greater victory
For the sake of independence and freedom
we need to make Americans go home and
make the puppet troops collapse.
My men and my people march forward
If the North and South unify
it will be the happiest spring.

The words surprised Reed. He had been told that the people were Communists, fighting for a type of government that would eventually destroy all of Asia. But the song spoke of something else, a motivation that he could understand even if it was not the one that was the goal of the leaders. "Uncle Ho," as the beloved leader was known, convinced the people that "Nothing is more important than independence and freedom." Whatever else he may have been, he understood what all people cherish, what motivated the American revolutionaries such as George Washington, Thomas Jefferson, and Ben Franklin.

Reed had hated Ho Chi Minh during the war. As he stood talking with the old man in the morning sunlight, he realized that he had to respect and admire his former enemy and those who were like him. Right or wrong, their motivations were familiar ones, at least some of their goals the same as he would have had if he had been a soldier in the Continental Army fighting the British occupation force.

Nghia was more relaxed than at their first meeting. He was waiting for Paul on his front porch, just as he had done the day before. The greetings were the same, though upon entering, Nghia's daughter brought him the bananas he enjoyed. It was hospitality for an old friend, not a new one.

As with the day before, the talk began with two former soldiers reminiscing about their service. Nghia had fought the French in the Red River Delta area from 1951 to 1958, was com-

missioned as a second lieutenant in 1965 when he returned to
fight the Americans. Because he had served in two separate wars,
he was a man who had proven his love for his country and was
thus held in great respect by the members of his community.

Nghia was also a gentle man, educated in a manner that led
him to use poetry as the primary means for communication.
Even his letters to his wife, intimate love letters and those trying to explain what was happening, had all been written as poetry. It was an important trait, as was his language skill, his affable
personality, and the use of correct language even when having
to deal with rude, coarse men in the field. These were reasons
he had been made the political officer of his unit, a man whose
job was to keep up morale, to be aware of what was taking place
in the field far from his own unit's battles. That was why he carried newspapers and other documents to help him. That was
another reason he was so respected.

Paul asked Nghia about the medals he had earned, a ques-
tion that delighted the old man. His personal triumphs were on
the battlefield, his body too broken to achieve any physical suc-
cess within his community after his return. He took great pride
in showing his carefully preserved uniform with the Southern
Liberation medals. He had won The War Awareness Medal,
Individual Service For Less Than Three Years Medal, Unit
Victory In One Battle Medal, 1967 Commendation Medal, Five
Year Service-Third Class Medal, Ten Year Service-Second Class
Medal, Fifteen Year Service-First Class Medal, and a Twenty Year
Service-First Class Medal, the latter being the highest award
given for service during the resistance. As his wife watched, he
put on his jacket and posed proudly while Paul took his photo-
graph.

Trying to include Mrs. Nghia in what had been a conversation between two soldiers, he asked her what she thought of his
bringing Nghia's diary home. Only then did he fully understand
how much some of the words meant to a woman who had only
faith to see her through a time when she did not know if her husband was still in love with her, still thought about her. He had
told her when he returned how much he loved her. But they had
been apart for years. Most of his letters never reached her. The
diary was the first witness to speak of his heart during their long
separation.

"I'm glad you have done this. It's a good thing. I've read the diary. Now I know for sure Nghia really cared about me and the kids all those years he was away fighting. And I'm thankful you kept the diary so well preserved."

Mrs. Nghia explained that she had been left alone with three young children in a province which was a primary target for the Americans and South Vietnamese because of the manufacture of military materials there. The area where she lived was bombed heavily. "It was extremely difficult to gather three children at three o'clock in the morning and run to the bomb shelter," she said. She explained that there were times when they would have to make the run three different times in the same night. The randomness of the attacks was such that usually they could return home at the "all clear" sound. At other times they had to race from their beds over and over again. The stress was intense, and the family's leadership should normally have fallen on the shoulders of the husband and father.

Paul thought that such violence must have been the hardest part of the war for her to endure. Friends were killed. Homes were destroyed. The people historically sought to avoid confrontation in their daily lives. The culture was a nonviolent one periodically forced to go to war against one invader or another, one political leader or another. However, he was surprised to learn that more difficult was dealing with the death of her husband.

Again, Reed was in shock. Then this wasn't the Nguyen van Nghia he thought? This was the impostor he feared the day before. This was...His hands flew up involuntarily in a gesture of frustration and confusion. Her husband was dead? But he was in the room. Reed didn't understand. The scar matched the identification photo. The...

"Back in 1968, the government sent a letter informing me Nghia had been killed," she explained. It was only when he showed up on their front doorstep two years later, very much alive, that she learned the truth.

Apparently, the confusion came around the time that Nghia's unit was in combat with Reed's. He was as healed as he could be from the chemical defoliant exposure, then was wounded in the stomach the day the Americans captured the base and rucksack. He was found wounded in the midst of the battle, dragged to a position where some of the other platoon members could safely remove him, then carried to an underground hospital. He was not expected to live, and when he did, his immune system was so poor that he contracted malaria.

Day after day, week after week, he was away from all daylight. The shelling could be heard in the distance, but there was no way he could defend himself if he was attacked.

During this time a letter was dispatched to Mrs. Nghia reporting her husband's death. The letter brought two shocks. First, there was the loss of her husband, a tragedy beyond measure for a couple deeply in love. The second shock had to do with the culture of the people.

There is a stigma against being over thirty and female in Vietnam. A widow who is thirty or younger is a desirable woman who will often remarry. A widow over thirty is shunned by the men seeking a wife. Because of her age, her husband's death also meant a future that would be no different from the present. She would work the fields. She would raise the children. She would lead a difficult existence, the only money coming from what little she could earn until her children were old enough to help. Even then, with their opportunities limited by their father's death, there was a chance they would marry and be unable to afford to help their mother. The rest of her life would be as bleak as the time of separation.

"In the period 1957 through 1968, this area was heavily bombed," explained Nghia's wife, Vu Thi Gai. "I was very scared, very frightened. When we heard the warning the Americans were coming, I took the children to the shelter."

"At night I felt very sad," said Nghia, speaking of the same time period when he was frequently too far from home to be able to help his family. "So far away from home. So empty."

"At night I would have dreams—nightmares—that he was dead," said Vu Thi Gai.

"Sometimes I would dream about battles," said Nghia. "It was very terrible and very fierce. Why did the Americans come? And why did I have to live like that in the jungle? It was a very hard life."

"Before going South, he was a very strong and handsome man," said Nghia's wife. "But after coming back from the battlefield, he was a weak and wounded man. The most important thing to me was that he was alive."

The return was more involved than they said. More than two million North Vietnamese hiked the mountain path called the Truong Son Range, though known to Americans as the Ho Chi Minh Trail. Most walked the narrow, rocky terrain barefoot. The tanks and heavy artillery used in the final attack on Saigon also had to traverse the trail. It was five hundred miles, filled with snakes and other dangers. Most of the plant life could not be eaten, and there were limits to the supplies that could be carried. The men were usually hungry, never able to eat as much as they needed while making the journey. Their throats were frequently parched because water was scarce. Often the water would not be clean, but it was easier to deal with the parasites than to die of thirst.

Under the best of circumstances, the soldiers became ill. Some were so sick that they had to stay where they were, being sheltered in makeshift hospitals which, if not adequately camouflaged, would draw an attack by a helicopter. The dead were buried by the side of the trail.

"It was rough, very rough," said Nghia. "We had to contend with extreme heat during the day, and cold in the mountains at night. There were all sorts of snakes, tigers, diseases, and dysentery. The Ho Chi Minh sandals hurt our feet, so most of the time we threw them away and walked barefoot. It was rough, and slow-going in some places. Most of the time we had no medicine. Some of the men contracted malaria. Some got really sick. Several of them deserted.

"They would run off in the jungle and get lost. They were eaten by tigers.

"This actually happened. We heard them screaming as they were being eaten.

"If you made it through all that in one piece, you had to deal with the B-52s. They were so big and destructive sometimes they destroyed entire units. They disappeared completely, nothing was left. The planes flew so high we couldn't hear them. We didn't know they were coming until after they'd hit. It was demoralizing."

A North Vietnamese soldier starting down the trail, well fed, with adequate clothing and supplies, would take about three and a half months for the trip. The return up the trail should have taken about the same amount of time. However, Nghia was far from being in good health. He was partially blind, not fully recovered from the wound, and could be given no assistance. He had to return with the clothes on his back. Neither food nor water nor medicine could be spared. He would have to use all his knowledge as a farmer, all the skills he had gained in warfare, in order to survive on the trail.

The American forces knew the Ho Chi Minh trail well. They understood the need to stop the key supply line, and towards this end they regularly attacked portions of the trail with napalm, defoliants, and bombs. Military units traveling the trail would time their meals based on when the Americans seemed to be flying the least. They used extensive camouflage when they rested so they could not be spotted from the air. But such survival methods were difficult for Nghia, whose weakness left him at greater risk of being seen.

Malaria was one of the leading causes of death for the men who traveled the Ho Chi Minh trail, and Nghia was no exception. He had several recurrences of the disease, forcing him to stop, to live with the chills, the fever, and the other horrors of the affliction. If he managed to reach food and water each day, there was some hope. If he didn't, he never knew if he would recover enough to keep moving or if he would die from starvation and thirst. All he could do was live from moment to moment.

Day after day he walked, some days progressing several miles, others barely moving a few hundred yards. The trip that had taken three and a half months when he was well ultimately took two years. His thoughts were of his wife and children, of the village where he might at last know peace. And when he arrived, his wife had long given him up for dead.

"When my husband came back home, I was very, very happy to see him again. I thought from then on, my family is unified. Now husband and wife and children could join together. It's a very warm and good feeling."

Almost as bad as the walk was his having to face the reality that he had nothing to show her that would prove his thoughts had been focused on her during the years of combat. The poetry that had been so important was gone with his diary. She would only have his word that he missed her. She would not be able to fully know his heart.

Until Paul Reed returned.

CHAPTER ELEVEN

Nguyen van Nghia and Paul Reed were scheduled to return to the battlefield where they had unknowingly first encountered each other. It would be the first time either man had visited the area since the war, as well as the first plane flight for Nghia. But before they left, Nghia wanted to show Paul how completely he accepted the American. He took Reed's hand in his, then began walking through the village, smiling at all his friends, showing off proudly.

Reed was uncomfortable. Two men holding hands while walking through public streets had a negative connotation in the United States. The implication would have been that they were lovers, and the knowledge of his own cultural interpretation made Reed nervous. His interpreter had to explain that Nghia's gesture was one of friendship and respect. He was making a statement to the men and women of his village that this American was honored; this American was special. Paul Reed was his friend.

The trip was to be a difficult one for both men. Neither had been to what the Americans called Hill 1064 (named for its elevation) in twenty-five years. Death had been a constant companion for both men. They had each lost friends in the battle.

"As I think back about my friends, it is very painful to remember," said Nghia. "Soldier by soldier, they fought the enemy and were killed. All of my friends were killed."

It was November 11, 1993, when Paul and Nghia traveled to Hill 1064. It was Veterans Day in the United States, and Paul recalled having traveled to Washington, DC the year before for a celebration of the tenth anniversary of the Vietnam Veterans Memorial. Now they were together, two soldiers, both veterans, each having fought on the opposite side of the other. "I couldn't think of a better day to face our horrid past," Paul said, speaking of Veterans Day.

The road was better than it had been twenty-five years earlier. The men were in a van that had little difficulty moving along the bumpy route. What had not changed was the appearance of the same valley through which Reed had once walked. It was called "leech valley," located in the midst of massive steep-sloped mountains. The nickname came from the leeches that inhabited the place.

Leeches had been one of the tormentors of the soldiers when they were planning an ambush. The leeches were large, about the size of part of a finger, and they would often burrow into a man's crotch area. Their bite was painless, but they could not be pulled off. Their heads would be severed in the action and the wound they made would become infected. Instead, a tiny amount of mosquito repellent would be dropped on them and they would die at once.

The leech was also a friend. Many of the men were infected by cuts, especially from the elephant grass they encountered. The grass was so tall that some men could not see over it and tough enough that they frequently had to use machetes to hack through it. It was also razor sharp. Cuts were frequent and could cause serious complications. The wounds would fester and a poisonous pus would build up inside—a condition known as "jungle rot."

The men soon learned to use the leeches on their wounds. They would place the leech over the pus and let it consume it. Because the pus was a draining poison, the leech would curl up and die, falling off and helping them heal. Leeches also had helped Nghia with the injuries on his walk. But the value of the creatures did not change the feeling of disgust and discomfort that came when traveling through the valley.

Seeing Hill 1064 brought Paul Reed a flood of memories and feelings, though little of the anger he expected. It had been twenty-five years, and for the first time he could accept that there had been a generation of change. In fact, Minh Nguyet, the attractive woman who had helped coordinate the visit, had not been conceived when Reed and Nghia had their encounter. Men were not yet traveling on the moon and walking in space. There had been drive-in movies, drive-in restaurants, and television sets capable of receiving only three or four channels in any given area. There were no VCRs, PCs, or mobile telephones. It was a different world now.

Now, the land was beautiful—the mountains, lush bamboo, and banana trees all freshly painted in shades of green. It was "cool" by local standards, the temperature only reaching 98 degrees that day, though the humidity was just as he remembered it. The air still felt as though he was trying to breathe underwater.

"I once heard that people either run to the source of their pain and suffering, or they run from it," Paul said. "I understood the principle behind that saying. In most cases we choose either to begin healing or remain in denial. To begin healing was probably the most significant reason for my being here now. I'm no longer running from my pain. I'm staring it in the face. No longer is it going to control me. I'm going to control it."

The memories came, though not as flashbacks and night terrors. Nghia's unit was dug into bunkers at the top, waiting patiently for the American assault. Some had climbed trees, using the additional high ground to make maneuvering more difficult for the Americans.

The sun had been shining brightly on that day a generation earlier, but the jungle foliage was so thick that the men were in darkness down below. It was a day when Paul was convinced he might die in battle, and he feared spending his last hours alive in leech valley. The only comfort came from a friend, Rick "Goon" Ortler, who was on his second tour of duty. He had seen a year's combat and was a better judge of what they would be facing.

Reed, terrified, shaking, fighting for enough control to be able to aim and shoot accurately, leaned over and whispered, "Rick, are you scared?"

He never did know what his friend thought. He was unsure whether the friend was lying to comfort him or genuinely relaxed with the danger. Whatever the case, Ortler calmly stated, "Hell, no, I ain't scared. I'll buy you a beer when we get out of this."

Reed had relaxed until the moment of battle, an experience that shocked more than terrified him. Explosions were every-

where. Men were wounded. Men were dying. Air strikes were
coming in so close that there was no way to be certain whether
the pilots were so skilled, the nearness of the bombs deliberately done to provide maximum protection, or whether they were
lucky and the next pass would see Americans killed by their own
air support.

When the air strikes were obviously assuring the safety of
the Americans, forcing back the North Vietnamese, Captain
Davis had one of the pilots do a victory roll to boost morale. He
had just dropped a load of napalm with devastating impact on
the enemy, so for the victory roll he circled around, swooped
down nearly to the bottom of the valley, then headed east toward the ridgeline, flying at treetop level, rolling the plane over
and over as he flew. It had been an exhilarating sight twenty-five
years earlier. That day, with Nghia, all Reed could think about
was Le Thang back in Tien Hai, a disfigured patriot with the mis-
fortune to be born on the wrong side of the world.

Nghia consulted a map, his poor sight making it difficult to
see the terrain as Paul did. The ridgeline seemed close at hand,
but Reed knew it was actually a five-hour uphill walk. Still, both
men were determined to move closer to where they had had
their encounter with each other and death.

There was a narrow, well-worn trail that was easier to take
than moving through the bush. The route was not direct, but
they would have needed machetes if they traveled the other way.

They moved slowly in ranger file. The area was no longer
deserted because of the presence of massive numbers of
weapons of war. Rice and fruit farmers cultivated the land that
had once held mortars, grenade launchers, and caches of ammunition. The last time Reed had walked the area, only men of
the NVA could be seen, and when they were visible, he tried to
kill them. The peace of the land made him slightly uneasy, as
though it was the ultimate camouflage for some hidden violence
he had yet to face.

The walk held more memories of the past. There was a
small, fast-running stream they needed to ford. It was no more
than thirty or forty feet wide and eighteen inches deep at the
outset. By the time they were part way across, though, the depth
had increased to three feet and the bottom was soft and sandy.

It was a perfect location for an ambush, the men having been slowed by the change in the terrain.

At first Reed started to panic, thinking of his lack of weapons. Then he focused on the changes of the present, not the memories of the past. In the distance were mountains shaded by the canopy of jungle foliage. Tall Johnson grass and other plants adorned the water's edge. There were green, broad-leafed banana trees from which the men once liked to eat. Even the water's coolness was a refreshing change for feet still sweaty and tired in the heat and humidity.

There had been a time when the water meant all the necessities and amenities of life itself. The water was for bathing, for drinking, for brushing teeth, for cleansing wounds, for cooling a brow made fevered by infection. If you lived when making a water crossing, the life-giving liquid would refresh you enough to continue.

Reed's existence had been fairly sedentary since the war. Though disabled, Nghia had been more active. As they climbed inclines that were often quite steep, Reed was quickly drained by the hot sun and the humidity. He wanted to stop, to rest, amazed that he had once conquered the same terrain with an eighty-pound rucksack on his back. However, with Nghia, a generation older, matching him step for step, he felt he would lose face by saying anything.

Soon he was certain he would have a heart attack or drop from heat exhaustion. He fantasized headlines in which he, at forty-five, dropped dead while the sixty-five-year-old Nghia mounted the corpse on his back and carried his body back to the nearest village for shipment home to the United States.

Finally, the two men stopped to rest under a bamboo thicket. It was dark, hot, and had a familiar aroma. It was the type of location both sides would use for taking a break, and each was likely to booby-trap it for the other.

Reed fought the urge to feel for trip wires, yet his instincts warned him that they might be sitting in a trap. Then he realized that Nghia felt the same way, though his fear was poisonous snakes. Using training they had not called upon in decades, each cautiously probed the area where they were sitting. Finding nothing to endanger them, they relaxed and talked.

"What was the most disturbing thing for you about life in the jungle?" Reed asked.

"The tigers," said Nghia.

Reed had forgotten the culture, the need for an unmutilated body in order to move on to the next spiritual level, whatever that might be.

The American soldiers handled their dead coldly yet carefully. "Bag 'em and tag 'em" was the standard approach. It was like handling a side of beef. The grieving was over or delayed. Death was another part of the day's work. They would note who was dead, attach an identity tag, then put the corpses in body bags which would be transported out of the area by helicopter. Eventually, they would get a proper funeral. Eventually, they would have a normal burial in the United States. And there they would rest.

The North Vietnamese could not deal gently with their dead. The conditions of the living and the lack of helicopter transport support made their desires impossible to fulfill. Burial was immediate, for there was no way to transport the corpses. There was no religious service, no casket or grave marker. Families would learn of the dead and hopefully receive some possession, but that was all.

The soldiers would dig a hole wherever they were. If the ground was soft, the burial would be deep, the corpse safe from mutilation other than normal deterioration. If the ground was hard, the burial would be shallow. The tigers would come by, sniff the newly dead corpse, and dig in the ground until they uncovered it. Then they would mutilate and consume it.

"These were your buddies you befriended all that time on the Ho Chi Minh trail?" Reed asked.

"Yes, they were," Nghia replied, lost in the memory. His face was pained. He had never gotten over the disfigurement and loss.

Paul had different memories. They were sitting very near to where he had spent his first night in the bush. He had never before experienced the jungle, never experienced combat. He was surrounded by bamboo and the vipers that lived in the plant. Mosquitoes were attacking constantly and there was nothing he could do to repel them. He also heard periodic gunfire—M-16s and fragmentation grenades exploding all around.

At one point Reed had suspected he would die. He was in no immediate danger at the time, though. He did not realize that in the jungle, the sound of weapons fire carries great distances. The fighting was between either Bravo or Charlie Company and some NVA soldiers probing the perimeter. But he was the new guy. For all he knew they were being overrun. Reed listened in on the platoon radio which shared a frequency with the unit engaged in combat. He heard the firefight and a voice saying, "Here they come! Get your stuff…get your stuff!"

He did not realize that the message was for the other unit a safe distance away. He grabbed his rifle, fixed his bayonet, jammed his steel pot on his head, leaped to his feet, and ran to the other men in the platoon. They were standing around, whispering among themselves, relaxed. Reed was terrified, determined to protect them since they had no idea of the danger they were facing.

That was when he discovered that the others *did* know what was happening. They were laughing at him, delighting in the idiocy of the inexperienced new guy.

Being in the area of some of the bloodiest battles Reed had experienced left the American with mixed feelings about what he was doing. The war was over. He had changed his feelings about Nghia through the writing in a diary. He had placed what he thought was his former enemy's picture on the corner of his computer monitor, then stared at it daily, thinking about the man, trying to heal through the knowledge he gained from the poetry.

Now he was in the place where so many friends had died. He was with a man who had far greater combat experience, had lost more friends, had himself been wounded in a way that should have left him dead. Yet Nghia was strong. His walk alone, half blind, along the Ho Chi Minh Trail for two years had proven how tough he was.

For some reason Reed needed to know all his feelings, all his experiences in the area. "Did you ever see any of your friends get killed by Americans?" he asked. And Nghia said that he had. The words were slow, the answer painful.

The men walked up a hill overlooking a cultivated rice paddy. Then they crossed a dike that was a hundred meters long and only a few inches wide. Finally, they were in the midst of where the greatest violence had occurred. In his mind, Reed thought that the land wanted to cry out, "The blood of your brothers was spilled and cries out."

There had been horrible battles on the ground on which they were standing. Reed felt as though it was sacred in some way, cleansed with the blood of young boys of both sides.

As he looked at the ground, he felt as though he could hear the land crying out to him. He remembered the screams, the pleading, the fear. "Oh God, I'm hit...I'm hit...Help me...MEDIC!...MEDIC!...Am I going to make it?...I don't wanna die...Please don't let me...Don't let me die!"

The sounds rolled up inside his body as though a tape recorder had been imbedded underneath his flesh. All around everything was serene. The area was a pastoral setting that would attract dozens of Sunday painters if transplanted to a popular park in New York, Chicago, or Los Angeles. But the plants that now bloomed had been nourished on blood. The soil had been enriched by the life force of Americans and Vietnamese.

Reed could again feel the fear, feel the hate. He looked at Nghia and momentarily fantasized a devious man. He envisioned Nghia taking advantage of Paul's being lost in thought in order to slip into one of the underground tunnels that still dotted the land like a subway system made for people only. He imagined planted weapons that would be brought out and used against him.

"This is where I got shot," Nghia said quietly.

And again Reed understood. Nghia's odd behavior was the result of emotions from the past, just as Paul's had been.

The two men began talking about the tactics of the war. Reed wondered how Nghia's men were able to find them so easily in the jungle. He discovered that the soldiers used the American weapons against them. Just as the helicopters brought superior fire power into an area, they also were so noisy that they could pinpoint the troops they were supporting. The concentration of sounds allowed the Vietnamese to anticipate American movement and plan their regrouping, fleeing until a more opportune time, or attack.

Americans were also noisy in the jungle. Many of the North Vietnamese had several years' experience moving in the dense brush where sound carried easily. The Americans rarely spent more than a year in the field. They did not learn how to be quiet, and the result was that they were easy to hear.

"How much assistance did local farmers give your unit?" Reed asked.

"My unit operated mostly in the mountains where no farmers lived and farmed. They weren't much help."

"When you were involved in combat, how did you know when to vacate the area?"

"The minute we heard and saw helicopters coming, we learned to expect much more, so we left."

"Was it difficult to fight at night?"

"We couldn't fight during the day because our forces were too small. The Americans had the firepower advantage. Nighttime was the advantage we had over the Americans, so we used it."

"What kind of difficulties did you encounter at night?"

"Of course, it's always going to be difficult at night. But to keep from firing on our men, we used white arm bands. This helped us see the man directly in front of us."

"What problems did you notice about your new soldiers?"

"The biggest problem with new guys was that they couldn't cook without making smoke. I knew how and had to teach them. This was a serious problem because American planes could easily spot us, which led to our being attacked. The second biggest problem was that a lot of them went AWOL."

Reed asked Nghia about the use of a political officer. His former enemy had held this role, working on the morale of his unit.

"Many difficulties had to be overcome. The political officer was the one who handled them."

Reed wondered about the morale. He mentioned that many of the American soldiers complained about everything throughout their tour of duty. They were patriotic enough to enlist or willingly go along with the draft, but they were not willing to fully adjust to the hardships they were all facing.

"Some did [complain] and some didn't. There was a lot of griping."

The talk seemed almost superficial, yet Reed was struggling with his emotions all afternoon. They had spent the day walking over a battle area, a killing field, where defoliants, napalm, and other destructive materials had long ago dissipated. Flowers bloomed, animals could forage, crops grew once again. The air was peaceful, the sounds of exploding bombs and rapid fire weapons now a distant memory.

As they walked and talked, the images from the past sometimes flashed through Reed's mind. At other times he was at peace. It was like having a chemical rush from the adrenaline followed by an emotional letdown as he remembered where he was, the year it was, and the fact that the man with him no longer was a danger.

Still Reed thought more of his own men, his friends, than the North Vietnamese soldiers who had so recently come to be human to him. He flashed on the happy times with men who were no longer alive. He flashed on the way they looked just before they had to be slipped into body bags. He remembered his anger, though this time he was not filled with rage. Wars had been going on for centuries. They were written about in the Bible. They were discussed on parchments. There was nothing for which to apologize. There was nothing to celebrate. Life happened, even there in Vietnam, and that meant it was not always happy, not always sad. Everyone experienced what they experienced, and then they had to move on.

Reed bowed his head and prayed for the men he had known who had died. He silently said their names, seeing their faces in his mind's eye. He had not personally known them all except by sight. Yet he knew that despite that, they were his brothers. Life among them had taken on a special meaning because they had to fight so hard to achieve it.

The men started back to the van in which they had been traveling. It was a two-mile walk back to the road. The crew that was accompanying them had returned earlier, determined not to intrude. Children, unaware of what was happening, crowded about the men as they had in the villages. Reed was a curiosity to the children. He was never an enemy to them.

Reed looked at Nghia, who was also lost in thought. Both men had survived lengthy wars. The Vietnam involvement was

the longest military operation the United States had ever un-
dertaken. It was a complete failure in that the enemy could not
be defeated within the parameters established by the United
States government and the leaders of the American military.
When it became obvious that it was time to withdraw from Vietnam, the North was able to move into control of the South.
We lost the war, though many politicians liked to declare that we
never were at war. We were involved in what was considered to
be a police action, assisting the South Vietnamese government.
But it was full-scale war, violent, bloody, and unwinnable by
virtue of the unusual culture. That the two men had lived was
remarkable. That they were able to get together as they had, to
become friends, to reconcile with one another, was to Reed
miraculous. He had hated too much for too long. He decided
that the healing was the result of the hand of God, and as they
were driven to their hotel—Kach San Pleiku—for overnight rest
before exploring some of the places where Nghia had been post-
ed, he realized that the healing had begun.

12

CHAPTER TWELVE

Paul Reed wasn't ready to settle down for the night at the
Kach San Pleiku (the tourist hotel in Pleiku). The last
time he had been in Pleiku, all he had seen were olive
drab army trucks and red powdered dirt. The Army
trucks rarely used the roads that residents normally used and
instead turned Pleiku into a dustbowl by driving on temporary
dirt roads. Paul's memories were of living in areas that the locals
would never consider making their home.

But the hotel was nicer than Reed anticipated. There was
even a laundry service which charged him only fifty cents
American to wash his socks, shirt, and underwear. The room
was comfortable, the drinking water had been boiled for safety,
and there was even an overhead ceiling fan that confused him.
Button number four in the U.S. would indicate high speed.
However, in Vietnam, it meant low speed. Chuckling, Reed dis-
missed this as yet another example of the differences between
Americans and Vietnamese. No wonder things were so perplex-
ing during the war.

He knew he should be rested for the next day's trip to An
Khe. But this night, it was the streets of Pleiku that fascinated
Reed. They were jammed with people—most of them appeared
to be peddlers working from roadside stands. Entrepreneurial
activity dominated the town, even though the population
seemed too small to support such street commerce.

Paul had been worried about the way he would be treated as
an American. To his shock, more than half of the people in the
city had not been born during the "American War." They were
unaware of what had happened except as a subject in their history classes. The older men and women were much like Nghia;

they felt that when it was over, it was time to rebuild their lives. Anger was not something to cultivate.

Many of the people studied English (the word on the street was that English is the key to rebuilding Vietnam), and Reed, trying to use the little Vietnamese he knew, was frustrated by men, women, and children flocking to his side to try and speak English. They were quite excited, and he felt as though he had just handed out ten-dollar bills when the people talked with him about America. It was obvious that many of them dreamed of moving to the United States. In America, "American Dream" means having things: a nice house, two cars, three TVs, and a good school for the kids. However, in Vietnam, the phrase means something entirely different—just getting there.

The variety of products being sold surprised him. One woman, old enough to remember the war, who used the English name of Wendy, sold tiny pigeon eggs from a small stand. Paul was intrigued by her cleverness, as well as by her success with such a seemingly odd product. She explained that she had to sell from fifty to seventy-five pigeon eggs a day to make a living, and apparently she was regularly meeting her quota.

Despite the unification, the southern villages and cities had people who greatly disliked Ho Chi Minh. He had become almost godlike to the people of the North, but his name brought only silence from the Southerners, most of whom moved away from Reed when he brought it up.

The other surprise was in seeing older women still chewing betel nuts. The betel nut was supposed to provide a mild "high" much like a recreational drug. It also blackened the teeth of anyone who enjoyed this "treat." It was a habit he thought might be carried over from the war years, for such chewing had been fairly common back then.

The next morning brought a mixture of memories that were not all painful. They got in the van and drove past the locations of Fire Base Schuller and Checkpoint 24, an area where Reed had been assigned for a month during the war. His job then (and that of the rest of his company) was to secure bridges the Viet Cong regularly tried to blow up along Highway 19. During one of their efforts they had successfully attacked Checkpoint 21, killing three Americans and wounding six more. The men knew that the assignment would bring them into less combat, but they were in constant danger of attack. Many times Reed watched helplessly as the enemy fired rockets and mortars into Fire Base Schuller. Americans died during such attacks, and men like Reed could do nothing about it.

The local people—the ones Reed was there to support— were nice, though. The bridge Reed was assigned to guard was directly across the road from a Vietnamese farmhouse. The man who lived there was a hard-working farmer, married, with three daughters and what Reed thought was a pet dog named Frag. They were so kind to him, he decided to have his parents send them a gift. He arranged for a case of canned sardines to be sent to them, something they dearly loved. In gratitude, they invited Paul to dinner.

There were many cultural differences between the Americans and the Vietnamese. An American man relaxing with his arms folded across his chest would mean nothing in the United States. In Vietnam, that gesture was an insult. It meant that you were calling the person with whom you were talking a liar. Another difference had to do with eating, for it was an insult if you did not eat all the food that was placed before you.

Reed cautiously accepted the invitation from the farmer's family, then was shocked to see how they lived. The five of them lived in a mud hut. There was grass on the roof, dirt floors, and no front door, only an opening from which strung beads were hung for a degree of privacy from the outside. The household broom was made from dry corn stalks, and the bed, as hard as if they slept on the ground, was covered with a bamboo mat.

The single room was divided so the bed was in one corner, the cooking area in another. The table was set when Paul arrived, and the meal was a simple one, hamburger meat, gooey rice, and raisins. Or so he thought.

Thinking the humble meal might be tasty, Reed started to take a spoonful of the rice, only to have the "raisins" fly away. It was covered with big Texas-size horseflies, to which the family was oblivious. Reed decided to settle for far less rice than he originally planned on and tried to calculate just how badly the family would be insulted if he didn't eat at all.

Then there was the hamburger meat mixed with vegetables, all of which had an odd taste. Reed gamely ate what had been set before him, then looked around and could not find the dog. "Where's Frag?" he asked, hoping to play with what he thought was the family pet. Instead, the wife explained that Frag ". . . go make GI stew." Reed sat stunned, trying not to think of his stomach.

An Khe had changed significantly. The shanty town in which the main commerce had been to find ways to take advantage of the GIs was gone. No longer could you buy drugs, women, and jewelry with equal ease. No longer was this a shanty town where the people were barely getting by.

Reed found the road that was used to go from An Khe to the 173rd base camp that served as his unit's main headquarters. This time there had been no progress except for deterioration. The dirt road remained, and tank tracks had so embedded themselves in the ground that they were still visible. A junkyard replaced a few houses, presumably the ones no one wanted. And everywhere there were the remnants of war. There were 81mm rounds of ammunition, tail fins from exploded rounds, tank parts, and other deteriorating reminders of the once vast killer machine. There was even a recycling effort of sorts, an old steel helmet having been converted to an oil drain for motorcycles.

It was ironic to Paul. The base for destruction was disintegrating much like his hatred for Nghia.

Some of the memories were humorous ones. The mess hall at this base used to close at six o'clock every evening. If you were late, the cooks (called "spoons") would refuse to serve you a hot meal. However, when grunts were late because they had been in the field for forty days, they felt that they were entitled to something more.

That was what occurred with Reed's friend Rick Ortler. Rick and a few others had been humping the bush for forty days. They were hot, tired, and vowed to never again eat out of cans except for survival. Base camp was supposed to be an oasis for them, a place where they could get good, fresh-cooked meals. Except that the mess hall had closed at 6:00 P.M., and at 7:00 P.M., even knowing the situation, the "spoons" refused to grant an exception.

Frustrated, standing heavily armed just a hundred feet from the mess hall, the men took their M-60s and hand grenades and attacked the building. The roof was blown away, the building badly damaged, but no one hurt.

Reed was asleep in a nearby tent. Suddenly awakened by the sound of machine guns, he grabbed for his weapon and moved swiftly, though carefully, from his tent to help fight the VC. That was when he heard the cooks cursing Ortler, who was delighted by his revenge.

Another incident had occurred in that same area when Reed's unit was still allowed to go into town. By February 1969, paratroopers of the 173rd were not allowed to go into any town, nor were they welcome in some of the fire bases. Their attitude and actions were rude, crude, and violent. They were like animals demanding whatever they wanted. The situation troubled the leaders, who forgot that the men were trained to be predators in warfare. They could not leave a jungle firefight, clean up at the fire base, and go into the city without carrying over the aggression, disdain for the Vietnamese, and the hatred that sustained them in combat. Apparently, the violence had become so widespread—bar fights, beatings of prostitutes, and the like—that by the time Reed was discharged, none of the men were allowed in town. But he had savored the village life long before that, making the mistake of eating in a restaurant that promised "hamburger, french fries, and Coke" for a very reasonable price.

This was food made in heaven. It wasn't the C-rations on which he had been living. And it wasn't the much better food of the mess attendant. This was junk food, pure and simple. It was just the meal to take his mind off his troubles and the dangers all around. Reed entered the restaurant and gave the server his order. Within a short period of time the man presented him with a Coke bottled in China, half-cooked potatoes, and a hamburger made from dog meat.

The frequent eating of dogs was not the result of near starvation such as happened when the people of London began eating horse meat during the darkest days of World War II. Instead, the Vietnamese looked upon dogs as Americans look upon pigs, as animals to be bred for eating rather than pets. The dogs were intelligent and friendly, making their care simple. But pigs are more intelligent and just as easily made into pets. Thus, the Vietnamese could never understand the revulsion felt by Americans, and the GIs never could bring themselves to regularly eat the full range of Vietnamese specialties.

Although the area around the 173rd base camp was allowed to waste away, there were other locations where, twenty-five years later, the American War had become a valued commodity. Artifacts were in great demand by collectors.

For example, in Bong Son, near Reed's old landing zone, people moved with metal detectors among grazing animals and densely planted fruit trees. In other areas they would find nicely dressed teenagers with hoes and other digging implements working the ground. All of them were seeking shells, bullets, rifles, pieces of armored vehicles, and anything else they could find. Then they would sell them to collectors among the people.

Some of the work was dangerous. Paul noticed a few unexploded artillery rounds among the finds. Yet no one cared. Of greater concern were the land mines that remained in the ground a generation after the war. These periodically were exploded by the teens and others, including men who had been specially trained for their removal. The hospitals had a number of patients who had lost arms and/or legs from the exploding mines. It was a sign that the violence might never end despite the battles long being over.

Nghia's diary contained a number of poems about the Hien Luong Bridge, which crosses the Ben Hai River, the natural dividing line between North and South, in the area known as the Demilitarized Zone (DMZ). This term is an odd one since it was one of the most heavily fortified regions during the war. It was roughly the seventeenth parallel and it divided the North from the South.

Tran Khanh Phoi, the Vice-Chairman of the Quang Tri People's Committee, met Reed and Nghia, taking them across the bridge that led to the Northern territory. There was a monument built to honor the liberation of the South. This was also an area much like some of the communities where the American Civil War was fought. Families and friends were divided. Soldiers often had friends or acquaintances on the other side. As a result, the soldiers would try to kill each other during the day when battles were raging. But at night, when all was quiet, the soldiers would move into the other's territory and share dinner together.

Reed had heard that such a situation occurred in the United States during the battles between the Union and Confederacy in towns where families were divided. He had always found that aspect of war quite unnerving. It was as though the men had agreed to kill anyone, even when they personally felt no reason to be at war.

Nghia, seeing the sign commemorating the unification, commented, "You know, we paid for the cause. But finally we got our independence [from all outside influence—Chinese, French, and American]. And we contribute our efforts in bringing, for other people, happiness. I don't think it's a worse thing. And in doing so, also bring about happiness for ourselves."

Reed commented, "It has relieved me to find out that he's [Nghia and his fellow soldiers] a lot like us. I found out that they had the same experiences we did. They had leeches and jungle rot. But it's been good to find out... It helps me to find out that they had the same problems I did.

"For a long time I had the concept that they didn't have the problems we did. But now... just by being able to talk with him and share with him and learn from him, I found out they did have the same problems we did."

"You know, at that time we [the Northern army] always thought [South] Vietnamese didn't invite any countries," said Nghia. "But when Americans came here, they were regarded as foreign invaders. We were determined to win over them and push them back away from Vietnam. And we also thought that after liberation, you could come back and see your family."

Standing at the DMZ, Paul Reed explained to Nghia how he had learned what he thought was the story of two totally separate countries—North and South Vietnam. He said, "The whole concept I had of the Vietnam War was that South Vietnam was a separate nation unto its own. North Vietnam was a separate nation. And the North was trying to take over the South. The North was the aggressor and I was here to protect the South from the North."

"At that time there were two different governments," said Nghia. "In the South, the South was occupied by foreigners. In the North we were taught we should liberate the South."

Reed remarked, "After I read Mr. Nghia's writings, [I realized that] they viewed us as the aggressor."

"I didn't even know what Americans looked like when I heard they invaded the South," said Nghia. He explained, as he stood by the bridge separating what had been the North and the South, that the first poem in his diary was not his own but that of a friend. The friend, who was killed in the fighting, was his inspiration to keep fighting. That was why he placed it in his diary where Reed thought it was written by Nghia himself.

> For seven years I have stood guard
>   at the seven-span bridge,
> So many times I have paced back and forth.
> Life overflows on the northern shore
> And spreads to the high sea.
> Oars splash to the beat of the rowing song.
> Why does the South so move us?
> On the southern shore of the narrow river
> The nights are dark and lifeless.
> I feel the crying of the people.
> I have met many sweet sisters on the southern shore.
> Their sufferings find me on the other side
>   of the seven-span bridge,
> Leaving me ever troubled.

Reed was left only with questions. The more he talked with Nghia, the more he respected him. But the philosophy of the Vietnamese, their determination to fight for generations, then to instantly move on with their lives after the war is over, is foreign to most Americans.

Yet Nghia has never forgotten the horrors of the war. "In my sleep, I imagine some battles which were very fierce. And I saw many helicopters and aircraft dropping bombs and many artillery charges."

He added, "You know, the war left behind me heavy losses. Because I lost my friends, I was wounded, I had many difficulties during the war. And now my health is not good. Sometimes I was sick because of my wound. And so, it's personal not for me [sic]."

The van took the men to Route 9 over toward the Ho Chi Minh Trail. Nghia began talking more about the experience. Approximately two million North Vietnamese soldiers walked the trail used to infiltrate supplies, weapons, and soldiers into the South.

The trail was not needed until after April 1965. Before that time, the NVA troops infiltrated the south by crossing the Ben Hai River on Highway 1. Then the U.S. marines landed in Da Nang, cutting off Highway 1 and turning them to the mountain range trail of Truong Son Range. The maintenance of the trail alone required 13,500 men. It ran south from Highway 9 toward the A Shau Valley.

Death was so prevalent on the trail that today the Truong Son Range National Cemetery is located close to the Ho Chi Minh Trail, seemingly in the middle of nowhere. Only a dirt road can reach this national monument. There are no towns close to it. But the cemetery is the resting place for over 14,000 of Nghia's fallen countrymen and women.

Near the middle of the cemetery is a shrine and overhead sign which translates to "The Homeland Takes Note Of The Fallen" (To Quoc Ghi Cong).

Quietly, Nghia began looking at the graves to seek the names of friends who were not so fortunate as he was. Seven hundred men from his province died, and it did not take long for him to spot some of the men with whom he had once battled the Americans. The graves that held a corpse had the name, date of birth, date of death, home province, a yellow star, and the words "Liet si," which translates roughly, "martyr." Other graves just had markers, the sign that their bodies were never recovered.

Nghia moved quietly, focused inward, looking much like the American soldiers making their first visit to the Vietnam War Memorial. Veteran after veteran of the Vietnam conflict carefully touches and studies the names, sometimes weeping, sometimes remembering. Reed wanted to say something, if only to show Nghia that he understood the emotions. However, he understood so well that he had nothing to say.

Paul Reed and Nguyen van Nghia spent eleven days together. Both men relived the violence and were exposed to a Vietnam neither had experienced before. Paul had come from Dallas, Texas, one of the largest cities in the United States. Nghia came from a village of five thousand people where everyone knows the lives, the sorrows, and the joys of everyone else.

Reed was not certain what he hoped to discover when he returned the diary he had obtained in Kontum Province. He reached his last day uncertain what he had found. All he knew was that he desperately needed to put the past behind him, to gain closure on a year in hell which had haunted his daily existence for another quarter century. He had wept. He had been terrified of his former enemy and he had come to love the man as a comrade in arms.

Oddly, the first time he noticed how much he had changed was in the restaurant where he and Nghia had dinner their last night together. The Thanh Lich restaurant in Da Nang, a short walk from their hotel, was international by design, the staff bilingual or multilingual, the food a combination of American, European, and Chinese dishes.

Reed explained he was an American to the delighted waiter, Tran Duc Vinh, who spoke a little English. The men ate and talked, and some time before they left, a woman came over and touched Paul on the shoulder. She was Vietnamese, young, beautiful, and curious about the American. Her actions were flirtatious, and Paul found her attractive though he did not even try to talk with her. But he did muse that it would be nice to simply enjoy the friendship of a charming woman. This was a change, a radical change, and he was delighted. He had thought about enjoying her company as a person, rather than demeaning or abusing her as he once would have done. He had seen a woman—a delightful person—rather than a female gook.

The next afternoon there was an exchange of presents. The Nghias, enjoying the way Paul loved bananas, gave him a quantity of the fruit. He took his silver paratrooper wings and pinned them on Nghia's chest, remembering the emotions he had felt when they were first pinned on his own chest after completing jump school. It was the most personal gift he could give Nghia, and the action was a means of honoring the enemy who had become his friend.

Reed also thanked Nghia for both collecting and writing the poetry that led to his return to Vietnam. "Without it, it's doubtful if I'd ever have broken free."

Then Paul stood at the van and said, *"Tam biet, hen gap lai, cang som cang tot"* ("Good-bye, see you again, the sooner the better"). The pronunciation was probably not quite right, especially the way Nghia laughed and shook his hand to say good-bye. But respect had been shown.

On the return, Paul Reed commented, "The war is long over, but it still rages in my mind. I've learned this is true for Nghia, too. Though he doesn't realize it, he and his family have suffered much. He paid dearly. He was blinded, shot in the stomach, not expected to live, contracted malaria, then told to walk home. He had no food, no money, no medication, and several malaria relapses on the way. Taking over two years to reach home, his wife declared, 'The government told me you were dead!' Because I had his ID card and papers, he couldn't prove his identity and his government denied him any compensation.

"Today for his dedicated service, the government compensates him seventy thousand dong (the equivalent of seven dollars in U.S. money) per month.

"I had never once considered the hardships of the other side, the hardships they had to endure. They are warriors. I respect the North Vietnamese soldiers for that. What I'll remember most about Nghia is that he is like me. Not necessarily wanting to, he did what he had to. We were both proud of our countries. We were just on opposite teams.

"I'll also remember the kindness of his family. When I left, he didn't want me to go. We had become friends. He was my first Vietnamese friend."

Paul Reed returned to the United States and began speaking of Nghia to friends in the VFW, to church groups, and to anyone else who would listen. The documentary was completed and began airing, broadening awareness of the story and winning honors for the filming of the emotional impact of Reed's experience.

Several men in Reed's unit decided to help Nghia. There is a chance that American surgical techniques can help improve Nghia's vision. Some of the effects from the defoliant will be permanent, and Nghia will never have full sight. But after hearing the story and seeing the documentary, the Vietnam vets decided to help a fellow soldier, even though he had fought for the other side. And perhaps in that there was a greater healing for them all.

Reed still has an occasional nightmare, still thinks about the war every day. The memories of death and atrocities will probably haunt him the rest of his life. But he understands war as he never did before. He understands the shared experiences of soldiers used by governments, each side convinced of its rightness, neither side really knowing.

In the Bible, the winning side ascribes the victory to God. Paul Reed was not on the winning side. The Americans evacuated, the South Vietnamese government collapsed, the North reunited the nation. Yet in returning the diary, meeting his enemy, and discovering both their inherent humanity, perhaps God did provide a victory for them both.

> *He will judge among the nations, and will rebuke many people; they will beat their swords into plowshares, and their spears into pruning hooks; nation will not lift up sword against nation, neither will they learn war anymore.*
>
> *—Isaiah 2:4*

> *You know, before I...thought...because my husband is often sick, and got wounded, he could not remember what happened very well during the war. But when we received information that his lost pack and American, named Paul Reed, and brought back the diary and other items...Our family was very, very happy.*
>
> *— Mrs. Nguyen van Nghia*

The Diary of
Second Lieutenant
Nguyen van Nghia

Translated by
Rick Murphy
and
Nguyen Dinh Thich

I t is always difficult to translate poetry from one language to another. Word images and sounds which flow artistically in the one tongue are likely to seem disjointed in the other. In this case, such problems are compounded by the radically different nature of the grammatical and syntactical structures of Vietnamese and English. *Phong ba bão táp không bằng ngữ pháp Việt Nam*, say the Vietnamese—"No storm rages like Vietnamese grammar." Vietnamese is a fusion of Chinese, Thai, and Mon-Khmer languages. Thus it has words from both tonal (Thai, Chinese) and monotonic (Mon-Khmer) languages. Differences in tone (indicated by diacritical marks above or below the words) can result in two entirely different words being spelled similarly. A careless hand (understandable in combat field conditions) might inadvertently omit one of these marks, resulting in confusion for the reader. Vietnamese words never change in number, gender, person, or tense. But the same word can have different grammatical functions and, depending on its use, many meanings. Meaning is also dependent on word order, which can render confusing the liberties taken by amateur poets. In addition, the system of pronouns (one of the most complicated in the world) is very difficult to render in English. Often, the translators' choice of English pronoun is little more than a matter of opinion.

Because of these difficulties, the reader should be aware that another translator might legitimately offer a quite different translation, even though looking at the same diary.

This translation tries for a middle ground between the most literal possible translation (which would conceal its poetic nature) and a freer translation (which would produce refined

English poetry and thus may not do justice to simple soldiers who sometimes labored to put what was in their hearts into appropriate words).

There is a long tradition of journal keeping and poetry writing in Vietnam, and it was not at all uncommon for soldiers to carry poetic journals during the war. Due to the fortunes of war, untold thousands of these fell into American hands. A few thousand were turned in to authorities and kept in classified files until well after the war. Microfilm of these (now destroyed) diaries currently resides at the William Joiner Center for the Study of War and Social Consequences at the University of Massachusetts, in Boston. There has even been a volume published which contains translations of some poems from these diaries (*Poems from Captured Documents*, by Thanh Nguyen and Bruce Weigl, Amherst: University of Massachusetts Press, 1994).

Lieutenant Nghia's little book was more a resource for his job as political officer than it was a diary in the traditional sense. He included in it poems written by several different soldiers as well as some of his own. Unfortunately, he can not now always remember which is which or even what was the significance of the entries of names and dates at the front of the book or the "dedication" at the end.

The following pages contain a reproduction of the complete diary and a translation of each page, even when the significance of what has been written is not clear. Note that the poems often extend for more than one page and that some of them are composed as though written by some other person—a sweetheart from home, a Southerner, etc.

"Memories"
(19)67

(month)
Democratic Republic of Vietnam
Hoàng (a man's name)
November 26, 1967
Dang (a man's name)

*Ngày 5, 3 đến:
Cho Đến Ngày :   13, 65.
Đêm ngày 29, 3, 1965.
Ngày 17, 7, 1965.
9, 30", 8, 4, 65.*

March 5 to March (?), 1965
nighttime March 29, 1965
July 17, 1965
9:30 April 8, 1965

[handwritten Vietnamese poem]

Tôi đứng đây đã bảy năm rồi
Nhiều lần bước chân trên khoang
cầu bảy nhịp
Những Buổi sáng tinh mơ
Sức sống trào trên bờ Bắc
gay một Chèo ngỡ nhịp Hồ Khan
Sao phải tranh Lòng nhớ đó
Miền nam.

Chỉ cách con Sông nhỏ
Mà Bến đò đêm Đêm không
Còn ánh lửa
Tiếng khóc nghe nức nở
quân tan.
Tôi đã gặp nhiều Chị trên
bên bờ Nam.

For seven years I have stood guard at the seven-span bridge,[1]
So many times I have paced back and forth.
Life overflows on the Northern shore
And spreads to the high sea.
Oars splash to the beat of the rowing song.
Why does the South so move us?
On the Southern shore of the narrow river
The nights are dark and lifeless.
I feel the crying of the people.
I have met many sweet sisters on the Southern shore.

[1] The author of the poem (one of Lt. Nghia's friends) is standing guard at the Hien Luong Bridge, which crosses the Ben Hai River, the demarcation line established in 1954 to separate North Vietnam and South Vietnam.

Lòng trăng khuấng Hương qua cầu
bây nhịp
Nhìn cờ Sao Trung cảnh
Nhớ me cười êm ấm
Bên Bếp lửa nắm Xưa dưới anh.
Sao lập lánh
Me nhìn con Thở oná nhớ
Cảnh chia ly .
Không qua Rồi Vì Trí 1 giây
Tôi tiếu Hành đứng đầu Song
ngọn gió
Cha Me giao cho Tôi đứng đó
Người Chiến Sỹ đầu Cầu
Người Lính Của nhân dân,

Their sufferings find me on the other side of the seven-span
    bridge,
Leaving me ever troubled.

Watching the Star Flag billow,
I miss my mother, her warm smile,
In the kitchen tending a fiery stove
On a starry night.
I recall the painful separation
Of a mother from her young son.
For not even a second have I abandoned my post.
I am here for my parents, braving the wind,
A proud soldier of this bridge, of my people.

Little Korean Brother

Oh little Korean brother!
Where is your mother?
Where can she be found?
Is there anybody left to ask about
The invaders and war everywhere,
The corpses strewn about?
Snow silently surrounds the villages;
The homes are in ruins and deserted.
Isn't that your mother,
Her white body swinging,
Hair drooping from her skull,
Dangling from the end of a rope?

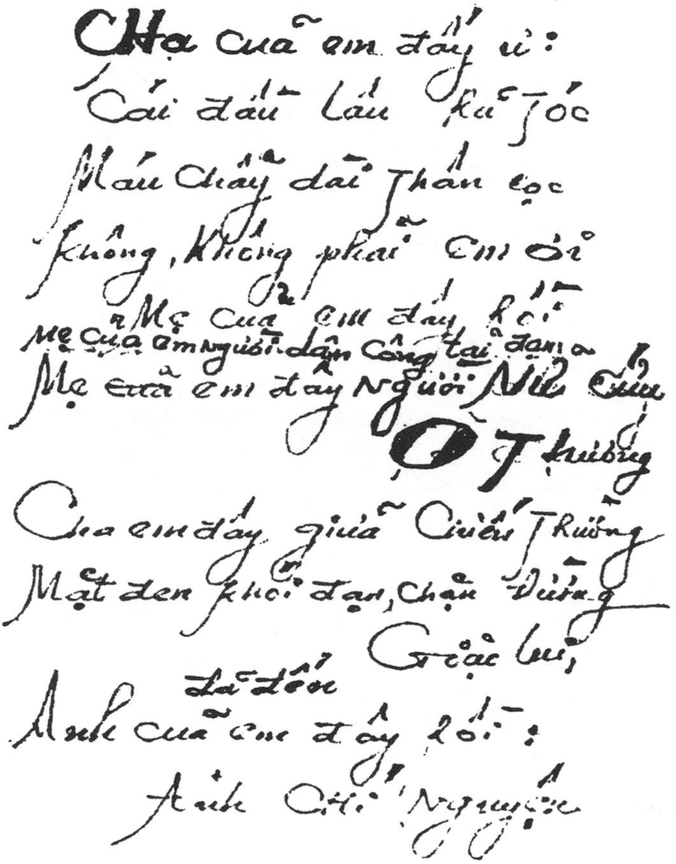

[Handwritten Vietnamese manuscript:]

Cha của em đây ư:
Cái đầu lâu xù tóc
Máu chảy dài thân lọc
Không, không phải em ơi
Mẹ của em đây rồi
Mẹ của em người dân công tải đạn
Mẹ của em đây Người Nữ Cứu
Ở Thương
Cha em đây giữa Chiến Trường
Mặt đen khói đạn, chận đường
Giặc lui,
Là đội
Anh của em đây rồi:
Anh Chị Nguyện

Isn't that your father,
Hair drooping from his skull,
His gaunt body covered with blood?
No, not so, my little brother!
Your mother is here
A laborer transporting ammunition
Here is your mom; she is a nurse.
Your father is here on the battlefield
Face blackened by gun smoke
Blocking the enemy's retreat.
Your older brother is here.
Your volunteer brother.

I am glad to be beside you, big brother.
Together with Father, we will slay all of the barbarians
So our motherlands can rebuild.
So our sisters can be happy
And sing in the meadows and rice fields.
We can live in happiness forever.
Today, little Korean brother, the guns are firing.
Tomorrow we will sing a new song.

Tôi Đứng Đây:

Tôi đứng gác đêm nay
Bên đầu Cầu Bến Hải
Giòng Hiền trong Xanh Một giải
Như mạch máu hai, từ Bắc chảy
Vào Nam.

Thảm Mạ Xanh Xanh in Trên
phù Hiệu Công An
Cờ Tổ quốc Trao Tay Mạ Hiền.
Từng phút giây nhắc Nhở,
Cha mẹ và Tổ quốc giao cho con.

I Stand Here

I guard my post this evening
At the end of Ben Hai Bridge.[2]
The steady blue current below
Is like a blood vein joining North to South.
Green rice fields reflect in my badge.
Our nation's flag was handed down to us
    by our loving mother.
Each passing moment reminds me that
My parents and native land
Have entrusted this son with the nation's fate.

[2] The actual name of the bridge is the Hien Luong Bridge. The author of the poem is referring to the Ben Hai River, which the bridge crosses.

[handwritten Vietnamese poem]

Standing before the gusts of wind
And the enemy's front-line,
Son, never forget.
Though seven years have passed
Remember all my advice:
Man your post proudly each evening
For the glory of the motherland.
Though the wind may howl and the rain pour
Keep looking forward.
Word has come over the loudspeaker;
We are to head South.
My beloved home village fades in the distance.

[handwritten Vietnamese poem in cursive script]

Nhớ đồng lúa năm nào jRíu hạt
nhớ những cô gái quê ta.
Tóc không Thế Vươn Tay hai
Giời đánh giặc giữ làng
Hẹn ai Còn giữ jRọn liên tìn
Nhớ Huế đầy nai Bình
Nhớ Tiếng hát Sông Hương
Mà. Trong quê Ta, Cóm
Chẳng đủ No, bữa đói
những đêm ghe tiếng Súng
Miền nam Vọng Lại
Nhức Sẽ Ruột gan nhức nhối

I miss the harvest season
I miss the girls of home
Hair longer than one's outstretched arm.
Now the girls valiantly defend our village.
Hue knows peace and tranquillity;
The Perfume River sings.
My native village knows hunger.
Every night the echoes of Southern gunfire
Tear at my insides.

[Handwritten Vietnamese poem, original manuscript]

From My Heart of Hearts

The enemy guns thunder
More madly with each passing moment,
Marking the fall of many of my friends;
They will never know life again.
The motherland weeps for them.
How can we possibly surrender?
We are the proud soldiers of the bridge,
Bearers of the Party's teachings.
We must silence the enemy,
Still them like glassy waters.

Tôi đứng đây giữ nhà máy
Nông Trường
Đang ngày đêm vươn mình Toả Khói
Cho tiếng quê Hương nguyện
Màu Lửa khói
Cho em thơ vùng Biển Tôi Thương Lý
Và đồng quê mãi mãi đón Xuân Sang
Việt hạnh phúc trên trăm Vùng
Sông Biển
Tôi đứng đây tạm thời phân chia
Giới tuyến
Nhìn Vào nam Bao giờ nhớ

<hr />

I stand here, defending factories and farms.
Day and night they bustle with activity
So the motherland will be blessed in wartime.
I stand here so my sister can attend school,
So our village can ever greet the new year.
I stand here at the demarcation line
Looking South, remembering North.
I am divided like the land.

Affection

My rifle firmly in hand
I cannot leave this land.
I love this land of the bridge's end
Where I have stood guard these seven years.
The pines of Vinh Linh tower upward forever,
I love the rows of folksy houses.
The wind unfurls the Star Flag.
Still, I miss the family hearth.
I picture the road of my native village,
A small lantern shining at each home's gate.

*Tình quân dân như Sidi ấm lòng
Tôi:
Tôi: ươm đất Nước kung còn
Giữ Tuyền người
Để cho hai miền trao Thương
Và Giữ nhớ!
Nước cắt Sôn nghé Tuyền
phú Xã,
Bột Sắn Tung Viện ngọt Bánh.
Chợ Chua.
Hồ kim môn ươt điểm
Tình Xưa,*

My troops by my side
Bring warmth to my soul.
I wish the country was no longer divided
So we could be together as friends
Enjoying the pure water of Son Nghe
The fishing boats of Phu Xa
Cassava cakes from Chua Market
Kim mon sweets imbued with the love of old,

The fish of canoes traversing Chau and Hai Thai.
But the Americans and Diem have partitioned us
Here at the Ben Hai River
We, the combatants of the bridge's end,
Remain always here
To thwart the enemy's advance.
Our faith is steadfast
Though by now it's been seven years
Since husbands and wives, fathers and sons
Have seen each other.
I stand here watching the enemy

[Handwritten Vietnamese text]

Forcing civilians to build bunkers.
Many the age of my mother and father labor at gunpoint.
Infants cry out to be breast-fed,
But the mothers must work.
Often I seethe with rage,
Chafing before the division of this nation.

Month after month I meet enemy soldiers
So how can I avoid sorrow?
We are of one blood, one race.
Brother, how can you be such a traitor!
The road you are on is full of blood and sin.

[Handwritten Vietnamese poem]

Không thể chờ đợi trong TV.
Tôi chỉ biết cuộc đời nho nhỏ
Hành và tiến như hạt kim cương
Tôi đẹp đẽ thành kho tàng quý báu
Đầy đổi hạnh phúc ngát hương thơm
Tôi chỉ muốn lời thơ êm ái
Bên tai tôi thỏ thẻ những chiều hôm
Tôi sẽ chút cả liên luyến ái
Hai tiếng cười bừng sáng muôn phương
Tôi chỉ muốn một chiều thu hây dưới
Trái tim người lao trai liềm tôi
Tôi sẽ đón cuộc đời trong gió sớm

I Cannot Wait in Vain

My darling, I can't take this anymore.
I only know my little life.
A diamond reveals its full worth
When shining in the darkness,
Inflaming sweet happiness.
I only want to hear poetry as the sun sets;
I promise I will be loving, faithful.
Our laughter will ring out in every direction.
I only want to watch the autumn sun set,
Your heart beating next to mine.
Our renewed life will arrive on the morning wind,

Theo mây về giớ Sớm Xa Xôi
Tôi Chỉ muốn một Mua thu êm ai
    Yêu và yêu mai không quên.
Tôi Sẽ đớn Tình yêu trong ước vọng
Tuôi đời mười đẹp bông hoa Tươi
Tôi Chỉ muốn Long có em dung đồng
Tình yêu tôi đã ngàn bớ Chia em Rồi
Tôi không thể đổi Tình yêu trong
                        tuyệt Vọng
Khi mặt nước Chập chờn còn cá nhây
Bạn bè Tôi tụm năm tụm Bây
Bây chim non bay lượn Biển khơi.

Once the clouds pass by.
I only want a pleasant autumn.
Love is forever and never forgets.
I will receive your love with open arms,
You are a beautiful flower at age twenty.
I only want your heart to belong to me.
Though we all too briefly shared love
It gives me reason to live.

The water flickers as fish jump,
By fives and sevens.
Baby bird sibs soar above the open sea.

[Handwritten Vietnamese poem]

Tôi giơ tay ôm nước vào lòng
Sóng mở lòng nước ôm tôi vào dạ
Chúng tôi lớn lên mỗi người mỗi ngã
Kẻ sớm, Rửa chài lưới bể đông
Tôi cùng bạn ra đi tập thể
Mà lòng tôi như mưa ngàn bão
Lòng nhớ về lưu luyến bể đông
Nhớ mãi có em đời mà ưng / trông
Thuyền em đậu Trong Lòng anh mãi
Em nhớ mãi những buổi chiều mai
Nắng vàng Ra mặt nước long lanh
Gió thôi mãi Lòng Tóc có em

I reach out my arms to embrace my country,
The surf embraces me.
We grew up together, then went our own ways.
One friend fishes these seas night and day;
My memories are like raindrops to the ocean.
Always, my love, I miss your rosy cheeks;
Your boat has docked inside me forever.
Do you remember the quiet evenings
The sunset reflecting on the water
The wind tossing your hair?

The breaking waves laugh in time;
Perhaps the water can measure time.
Please keep track of our memories.
We said good-bye, now we are apart.
The boat has taken my girl home.
That evening my heart writhed in pain.
I love, I suffer.
Her boat still parts the evening waters.
Darling, forget me not.
Be happy during your spring years.
Be sad no longer, lest my heart irreparably break.
Always remember our promises

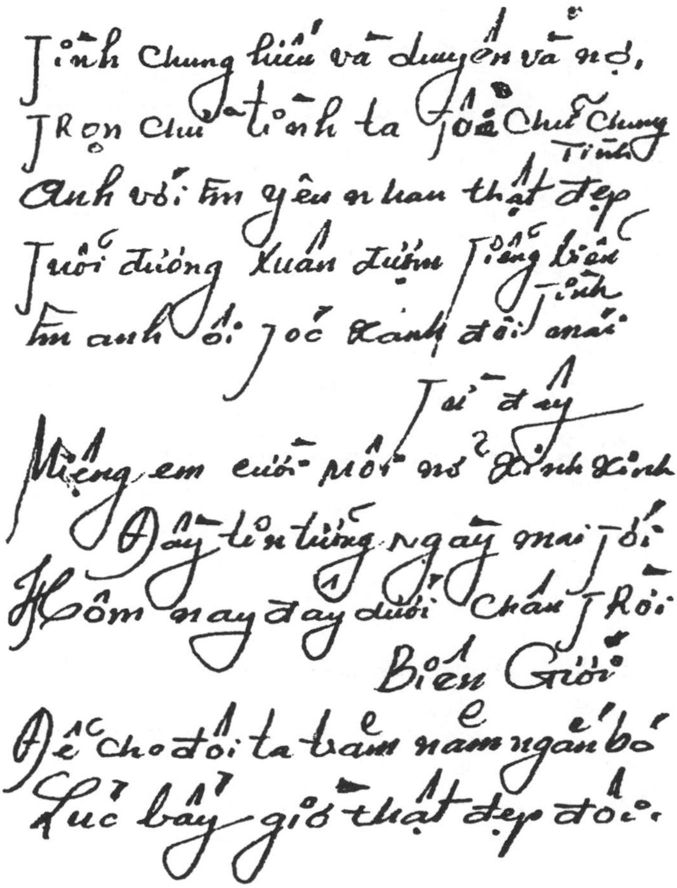

[Handwritten Vietnamese poem in cursive script]

Tình Chung hiếu và duyên và nợ,
Trọn chữ tình ta Hòa Chữ Chung Tình
Anh với Em yêu n hau thật đẹp
Tuổi đường Xuân đượm Tiếng liên Tình
Em anh với Jọc Ranh đời mãi

Tại đây
Miệng em cười một nụ xinh xinh
Đây lên từng ngày mai tôi
Hôm nay đây dưới Chân Trời
Biên Giới
Để cho tôi ta băm nam ngàn bó
Lúc bây giờ thật đẹp đôi.

To be faithful and forever in love.
Our love is truly wondrous;
Our hair will turn gray together.
You smile, your lips blossom with
Hope for tomorrow.
Today, on the border, I take in the horizon;
Believing tomorrow will come.

[Handwritten Vietnamese poem]

Gửi Mẹ !!

Xuân sang con gửi thư về
Chúc mừng tuổi mẹ sau thăm quê
Mừng xuân hẳn mẹ chờ
Đường mong mỏi đứa con xa chưa về.
Đón xuân nhớ mẹ nhớ quê
Mừng xuân con viết thư về, mẹ vui
Xuân về hoa nở nụ cười.
Tô hồng càng thắm nụ cười càng
xinh
Xuân về con đã trưởng thành mẹ ơi
Xuân về miền Bắc sáng ngời
Đang vui kiến thiết cuộc đời nở
Hoa.

To Mother

Spring[3] is here, your son[4] writes
To wish mother good health, good cheer,
Happy New Year.
The road of hope that would lead your distant son home
Has yet to be paved.
Spring is here; your son yearns for
His mother and native village.
Buds burst to greet the new year;
Love spreads as the blossoms smile.
Spring is here
Your boy, dear mother, is now a man.
The North sparkles in the new year
Growing happier as the flowers bloom.

Vang lên tiếng hát Câu Hò
Xuân về mang lại cơm no áo lành
Nhịp cầu đường Sắt tiến Lên
Xuân về ngọn lửa đấu tranh
Xuân về con mẹ vẫn chưa về
Vì con mang nặng Lời thề
Xuân về con vẫn ở nơi đây
Hay xưa Câu hát đón ngày Xuân
Sang
Đón Xuân nhớ Mẹ nhớ quê
Mừng xuân con viết Thư về cho Mẹ
Vui

The river below the bridge sings with renewed vigor.
Spring brings food and clothing
New railways
The new year stokes the fire of resistance
But leaves your son far away
For your son clings to his oath.
Spring is here, your son is still here.
Toasting the new year
Though missing his mother and home.
In the spirit of spring your son writes this letter
Wishing you happiness, Mother.

[3] The arrival of spring coincides with the (lunar) New Year for Vietnamese.
[4] There are no "I" and "you" pronouns in Vietnamese. The translation of this poem seeks to capture that. As it would be non-standard English not to use "I" and "you," they are used throughout the other poems.

My life is the army;
You are married to a soldier.
Lying here I miss you,
Aching throughout this winter night.
I cannot contain my desire to come home
As my annual ten-day leave draws near.
Sighing I count the days,
Pining for each next one to come.
The colder the wind, the more I miss you.
Lying here this winter night, who can I tell all this to?
Midwatch, morning watch...

[Handwritten Vietnamese poem in the original manuscript]

Đêm nào thao thức canh dài Hòn
   Canh —
Càng suy nghĩ kỹ càng thêm mong
   nhớ
Ai thấu chăng cho vợ quân nhân
Đêm nằm than thở cùng trăng
Càng suy nghĩ kỹ càng sầu càng
Bạn nữ cùng tuổi thanh niên
Người ta còn bé còn bồng
Mình thì cũng lấy chồng mà
Vợ chồng họ kể cày người cày
Lúc ngủ cũng lúc dậy có nhau
Họ thì nhớ cày bồ câu
Mình thì thui thủi đi đâu một mình

Sleepless nights pass, each watch grows longer.
Thoughts of seeing you still consume me.
Who can stand this war, this kind of life
I find myself lamenting to the moon.
The more I think about you, the greater my sorrow.
We have missed out on so much.
Friends our age have raised families by now.
I envy them so, husband and wife
      working side by side each day.
They go to sleep, then awaken to the sight of each other.
They are like pairs of white doves.
While we each go our own lonely way.

[handwritten Vietnamese manuscript]

I dream the resistance has won peace.
I lie next to you, whispering your name.
But you don't answer me in my deep sleep.
Suddenly the rooster crows in morning watch;
We are both alone again.
My head clears, I again painfully realize
It will be many months before I see you again.
I resign myself to endure to the end,
Until the country is reunified.
So I can come home.

Ru Con.

Ngày rồi tháng lại trôi qua
Năm 12 tháng có 30 ngày
Em ngồi bấm đốt ngón tay
anh đi ngày ấy đã tày 6 năm
Trời Xuân xanh ngắt mà hồng
Trời Xuân ngày ấy đang Tươi Lâu rồi
Quá trình thay đổi cuộc đời khác
Trải qua kháng chiến trường kỳ Xưa
Lá này rụng xuống đời đi mấy lần
Ở nhà em vẫn chuyên cần gia
Sáu năm kháng chiến vừa qua

A Lullaby

Days then months pass
A year is twelve months, each with thirty days.
You sit, numbering the days.
Fully six years have passed since I left.
That day your rosy cheeks were flush with youth.
Their brightness still warms me.
The good old days lapsed into
Ongoing struggle.
At home you still try to stay busy
Autumn leaves have fallen six times since I left.

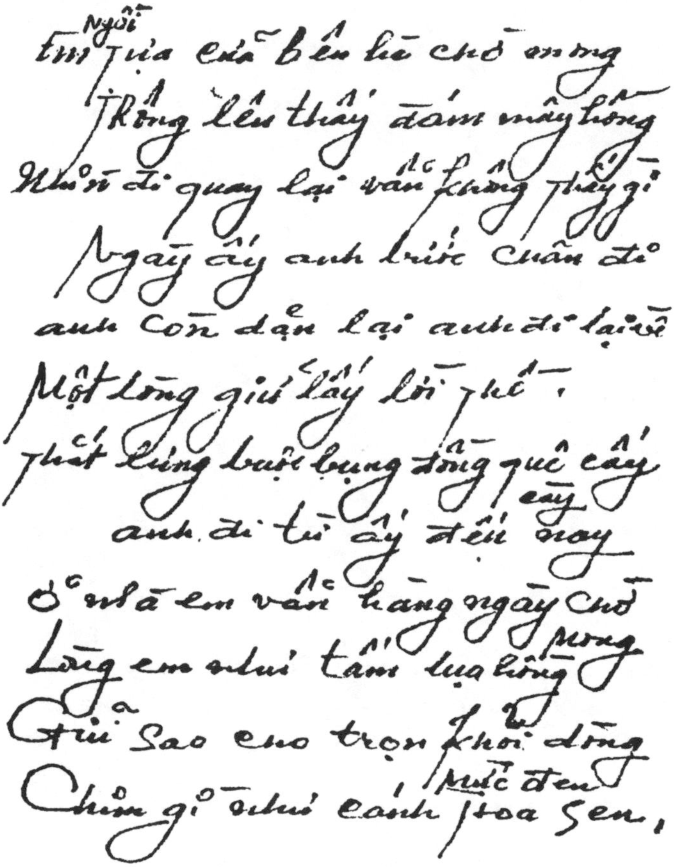

[handwritten Vietnamese poem]

You lean against the door, facing the river hoping.
You lift your gaze to the rosy clouds overhead.
You look 'round the yard hoping
But still see nothing.
The day I left I promised
That I would return.
I will keep my promise.
You've lost yourself in tending the rice fields
Since the day I left 'til now.
At home you are still daily hoping;
Your love is like pink silk.
How can I write all that I think of you?
You are a bird, feathered in lotus petals.

What could be brighter than the glow of us together?
The greatest love is yours.
As I lean against this light pole during midwatch,
I gaze at your picture and return your smile;
So sweet is your expression.
Our love is like the sunrise
Shedding light through rosy clouds.
Missing me you think up some verse
With this pen I will jot it down.
I am awkward; I don't know what to say.

How will I finish this letter
My heart is bursting.
Though far apart
The distance does not separate us.
We remain joined
In the spring of our lives.

[handwritten Vietnamese poem]

Chiếc đàn Môi.

Đêm qua Bên lửa Hồng anh thức Thâu đêm
Làm đàn môi Tặng người Thương
Hẹn nhau ta đợi Chờ anh nắm tay em
Nhìn mặt anh cầm đàn môi em

Muốn đánh hoài
anh ơi đàn Môi đây đàn Môi
này, làm lưu tin thầm
Gửi gắm ngàn tình thương Là
Dù Xa Xôi, Lòng em mãi đợi chờ 2 lần
Em bắt anh ở nhà Thương muốn
Cho đi Rồi Bản Thương Rồi...

The Flute

Last night beside the fire I stayed up all night.
I made this flute for you, my love.
Until we meet again,
May you see my face each time you play.
Remember our promises to remain forever faithful.
I can see you playing the flute constantly.
Though far apart, you will always be waiting for me.

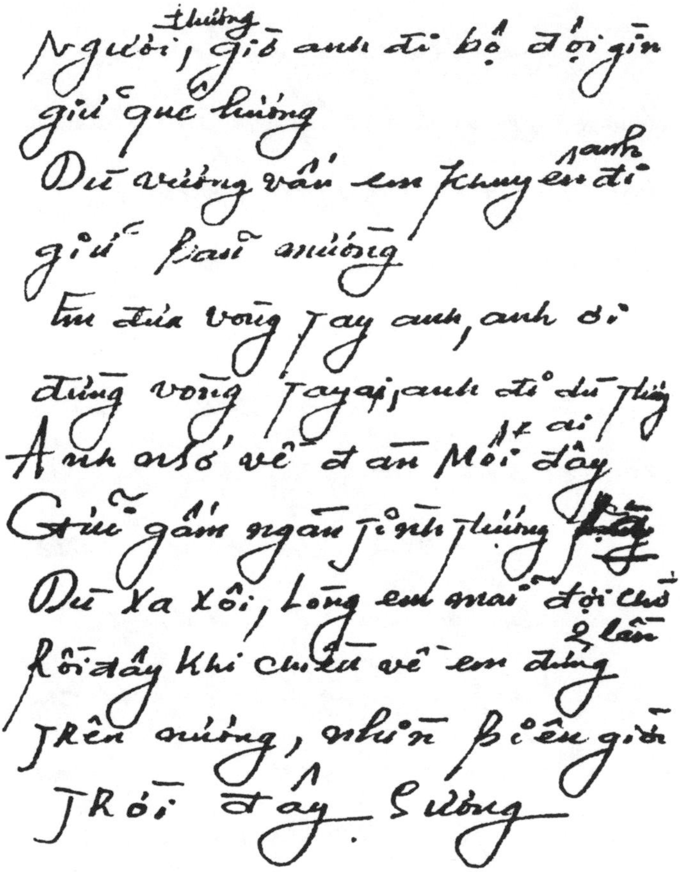

[handwritten Vietnamese text]

Người, giờ anh đi bộ đội gìn
giữ quê hương
Dù xương vấn em khuyên anh đi
giữ biên cương
Em đưa vòng tay anh, anh đi
đừng vòng tay ai, anh đi dù phải
Anh mà sẽ về đan mối đây
Giữ gắm ngàn tình thương
Dù xa xôi, lòng em mãi đợi chờ
Rồi đấy khi chiều về em đứng
Trên nương, nhìn biên giới
Trời đây. Sương

My love, you joined the army to serve your country.
Troubled, I yet advised you to go defend your native land.
We embrace, oh my dear
Never embrace another.
Please always remember the flute you gave me.
Remember our promises to remain forever faithful.
Though far apart, I will always be waiting for you
I stand here in the rice fields at day's end;
Mist clouds the horizon.

[Handwritten Vietnamese poem, reproduced in the author's hand:]

> Đàn môi bay liền hoa
> Theo gió bay xa.
> Em gửi Tới tình người Thương
> Xa cách dặm đường
> Lúa reo mừng Rên ruộng
> Mưa Đông Về, Lòng em mong
> Dệt áo dệt Tình Thương
> Tặng anh Xa Xôi
> Lòng em mãi đợi chờ
> Dù Xa Xôi Lòng em
> Mãi đợi. Chờ?

My little flute melody
Has been carried off by the wind.
It is for the one I love
Miles and miles away.
The rice shouts with glee in the fields
The blooming flowers renew my hope.
I sew this shirt with my love
To send to my faraway soldier.
Though far apart
I will always be waiting for you
I am always with you.

Cô Thợ Hàn

Ngước Trông Lên Lò cao
Ánh Lửa Hàn Loé Sáng Hơn Sao
Tôi ngước Trông Lên Lò cao
Thấy cô thợ hàn đan mắt
Trông Sao
Ngày nào Trên Tay cô cặp Sách
Chiều về cô vui chơi Thoả Thích
Cô vẫn Say Mê Sem Bác thợ Hàn
Kìa Xem bông Hoa đang nở Sáng
Mai chửi nên đổi fui Mẹ mắng
Miên man Thấy Trong
Lòng Rực ánh Lửa Hoa

The Glad Blacksmith Girl of Thinh Truong

I look up at the tall furnace
Welding fire brighter than the stars
I look up at the tall furnace
And see the blacksmith girl
Looking up at the stars.
Daily she returns home, satchel in hand
To enjoy a pleasant afternoon,
Still doting on her blacksmith mentor.
See her watch the flowers bloom in the morning
So absorbed in the moment
She must be scolded by Mom.
Brilliant flames well constantly from the depths of her soul.

Đêu nay mai Trên Lô cao
Ánh Lửa hàu Loé Sáng Hơn Sao
Đôi mắt cô đang mơ Sớn Sao
Ngắm Xem đừng Hàn mồ cân
 bóng cô yêu

Ngày ngày Tay cô Đùa mai
 miệt
Lô ngày mai Sớn mền mẻ phép
Cô Thấy vui phi đất nước
 Mạnh dàu

Đời Vui Lên bông Hoa nở Sáng
Mùa Thi đua cô hoa hồng phầm
Lô cao ánh Tương Lai đẹp Tửa
 Ngàn Sao !

These find the tall furnace,
Stoking the welding fire to brighter than the stars
That the blacksmith girl has fixed her eyes on.
She admires the stars as she does the fine welding line
That she so loves.
Day after day the girl's hands are busy,
For every tomorrow the furnace yields a fresh batch of steel.
She feels happy, watching the country grow stronger
Flourishing like the morning blooms.
At exam time the girl is a bouquet of fresh roses
The tall furnace makes the future as bright
As the countless stars.

Returning North to Visit Home

The dirt road leading home is vermilion red,
Ablaze like my soul.
Wind teases the green rice seedlings
Corn on the hillside sways gently in the breeze.
The banyan tree in front of the coffee shop
Recalls the days when I was young.
The mossy lake with the long bridge
Recalls the evenings spent fishing.
Thatched cottages, bordered by areca and bamboo
Line the banks
Along with jackfruit and banana trees.

The echo of peoples' voices resounds
    from the empty ferryboat
As the pigeons' coo lengthens.
But the charm of the moment is lost
In a homeland that stands divided,
In the heart of a separated lover
Who grieves for his broken country.
One day of love spared for the motherland
Is worth a hundred years remembering
The roof on one's home.

[handwritten Vietnamese poem]

Spring is Coming

Spring is coming, see the beautiful landscape
Spring is coming in sweet-smelling blossoms.
Merry butterflies alight on peach branchlets
Undisturbed by the wind, they hail spring's arrival.
Spring is coming, my heart grows warm
I think fondly of my young friend far away
In the spring of her life
She is like the golden moon rising in the sky.
I remember our love; I cannot forget
For a thousand years it will be etched on my heart.
I still await the reunion

Of a youthful wife and husband, mother and son.
But out of duty to my country
I remain out here, defending the hamlets and villages.
Spring is coming, millions of people are eager to share
Golden sentiments.
Spring is coming, I wish you good health, my love.
Please stay fully true to that which you love.
As you add another choice year to the spring of your life,
Bridle your spirit for the country's sake;
So there will be light for the full moon
So the lotus blossoms will be filled with a sweetness
Matched only by our love.
Far from you, my pen is my voice
Spring is coming, I send my rosy-cheeked lover a kiss.

[handwritten poem in Vietnamese]

Tình yêu

Là tình yêu Hãy đừng Dằn dỗ
Phải Đâu Là Con Bướm Với Cành Hoa
Đã yêu phải Tận đến già
Đừng Đùa Bởn Để Người Ta Đau Khổ
Là tình yêu Hãy đừng Nên Vội và
Để Có ngày Nên chóng yêu thương
Phải Cân Nhắc đi cho kỹ Đã
Là tình yêu Hãy Đừng Nên Xí Xóa
Nhắm mắt đi Mà quên cả cuộc đời
bình tình Lại Nghe Lời Tuyên ngừ
Là tình yêu Hãy Đừng Nên đến đỗ

Love

Love bears no grudge.
It is not a butterfly and flower,
Love endures until old age.
Do not trifle with love, or there will be sorrow.
Do not rush love
In order to enjoy it.
Handle love with care;
Be compromising.
Close your eyes, forget about everything.
Calm yourself, listen to the world speak.
Love bears no grudge.

Phải đâu là câu chuyện tình hàng
Đừng sáo nên đẹp để của tâm lòng
Vui chốc lát để ngàn đời như nhã
Những giọt phố cũng đừng nên lệ qua
Ừ cho mình dưới mắt của phàm
Kẻo già nửa là đời kẻ vô Duyên Tiên
Mà rút cục Hoa tàn trong khớn lá
Này bạn Tình yêu là cao cả,
Phải chung vô Thành Hạn chô cõi Thịnh
Mà thanh niên thế Hệ sau Duyên
Tình yêu lành mạnh chô vô yêu Tình
Và ngã Thước khi yêu Sẽ dâu
Mình Thư Thả:

Love is not a quaint flower arrangement.
Don't put on airs; act from the heart.
The price of fleeting joy is eternal shame,
But in saying so, do not be close-minded.
See yourself as adored by immortals
Lest you age ungracefully,
Finally to decay with the fallen leaves.
May you exalt love.
Be forever faithful; do not trifle with love.
Show the way for the younger generation.
Do not treat romantic love casually,
Lest it consume you.
Handle love with care.

To My Distant Lover[5]

Today, amid the fresh spring
We are far apart but still one
In the faith of our youth.
I remember your hearty speech and laughter,
The bright moon rising in the East.
Water running downstream past the wild grass.
The peach's freshness kindles my dreams.
Near you, form truly meets shadow
During long nights, yearning for you
I cling to our vows
Though we cannot live as an ordinary couple.

[5] The author again is taking the role of his wife.

Ghi lòng tạc dạ chớ phai
Trăm năm ghi lại một điều tạc chung
Mấy dòng chữ nhỏ ai ai nhớ
Nhớ bao nhiêu phải biết bấy nhiêu
Chắc anh không muốn nói nhiều
Mối tình giang dở trăm điều đắng cay
Thôi em viết đến đây ngừng nghĩ
Ngọn bút viết như và dòng lệ
Bài tìm này không thể nào nguôi
Cùng nhau giữ sổ một lời
Dẫu rằng biển cạn
Cùng cười bên nhau

May your faithfulness never wane.
For a hundred years, meditate on the word "faithfulness."
The letter-lines refresh our memories
There is so much to remember.
But surely you don't want to dwell on
Our unfinished love, provoking deep bitterness.
I must stop writing for now;
The pen's nib flounders in my tears
My heart can't be stilled . . .
Together, let us keep our word.
Though the seas may dry up
May we again laugh together.

Song to Sew Uniforms By[6]

Our soldiers are exposed to rain and sun.
The rain chills their insides; the sun burns their skin.
From cloth we fashion uniforms;
Our soldiers are resolved to exterminate the enemy.
My guy fights zealously on the battlefield;
Your gal swears to give her all.
Be quick of hand, brothers and sisters!
Looms whir, gunfire crackles through the green forest.
We fashion our hatred into poems.
Gunfire rhymes with the looms' whir.
We exterminate the enemy to the rhythm.

[6] This poem is written from the perspective of a girlfriend back home, sewing uniforms for her soldier boyfriend.

Ja may áo này Sao Cho kỹ
Cho giai phóng quân Vừa ý Đẹp
Ở manh Jay Lên nào anh Chị Em
                              Lòng
Áo may Song Mùa đông đã đến rồi
Giữ Chút Jình Jhương mến Vễ
ao Xếp ngăn Chú anh giải phóng
                    Anh
Lòng Vui Súng Vui đạt Lao
Ja may áo Sẽ đưa Ra ngoài tền
Chiền Jhương
Ở manh Jay Lên nào anh
         Chị em ơi
Ở manh Jay Lên nào anh Chị
         Em ơi ?

We sew these uniforms with great care,
For the satisfaction of the liberating soldiers.
Be quick of hand, brothers and sisters!
We fashion uniforms; winter draws near.
Proffering fresh new uniforms to you, liberators
Gladdens our hearts and brings us fulfillment.
We sew uniforms destined for the battlefields;
Be quick of hand, brothers and sisters!

The Southerner's Homeland

I hail from the South
Land of blue-green coconut forests,
Land of winding rivers
My homeland is stranger to hardship.
But after nine years of animosity,
I am determined to carry on the struggle
Until peace and happiness can be heard in
Singing birds returning home
Golden rice rustling in the paddies
Boat wakes splashing on glad rivers
The wind carrying the rower's song.
But how can the South Vietnamese

Dưới quyền của đối phương
Dân còn vui hát ca, Tay quân thù
Đầm sưới,
Xóm thôn Buồn âm thầm nát tan
Thu Sốt Sa.
Nhân dân nguyện đồng Tâm
Đấu tranh Lòng Vững Tin
Tương Lai rồi Thống nhất
Bắc nam Chung bóng cờ
Thiết Tha muôn Lời ca, mai đây
Rồi Miền Nam đồng Lai Nữa
Nước Xanh.

Under enemy rule
Be so full of song?
Hands covered with our blood
Their hamlets sadly silent,
Writhing pitifully in the hate.
The people struggle for a single nation;
The future holds unity.
North and South will share the same flag.
Tomorrow we will sing a thousand songs together.
The South is shimmering rice fields,
Abundant blue waters.

Nghe thuyền vui bến sông
Quân dân về chung sống
Sẵn khoai thêm mần tình
Thoả bao ngày ấp ủ mong.
Hai năm tạm biệt ly.
Bắc Nam cùng đấu tranh
Xây nên đời tươi sáng
Như cánh chim ấp ủ
Tháng ngày hướng
Nhớ về miền Nam

Listen to the boats rock, moored happily on the river.
Troops and civilians live together
The harvest grows more bountiful
With the peace and joy.
For two years I have fought here in the South;
One day North and South will fight together.
To build a bright tomorrow.
As a bird finds her way above the forest,
The days and months will find peace in the South.

Thân tặng Đ.C.

Đơn Vị Dân Quân T.Đông.

Tặng đồng chí Hữu khi lên đường
làm nghĩa vụ quân sự.
Đồng chí mang theo tinh thần chiến
đấu anh dũng để xứng đáng là
Người tiên tiến trong Quân Đội
Nhân dân việt nam

T.Đông Ngày 8- 4 -1965.

Warmly dedicated to Comrade Huu
T. East Unit

Dedicated to Comrade Huu, on the occasion of his departure
for fulfilling his military duties.

My comrade, carry with you a valiant fighting spirit. Be
deserving of your charge: a pioneer in the People of
Vietnam's Army.

T. East, April 8, 1965

> Hợp Tác Xã Việt Hưng
> Mường Phăng
> Huyện Điện Biên
> Lai Châu

Viet Huong Cooperative
Ward Phang
District of Dien Bien
Lai Chau City

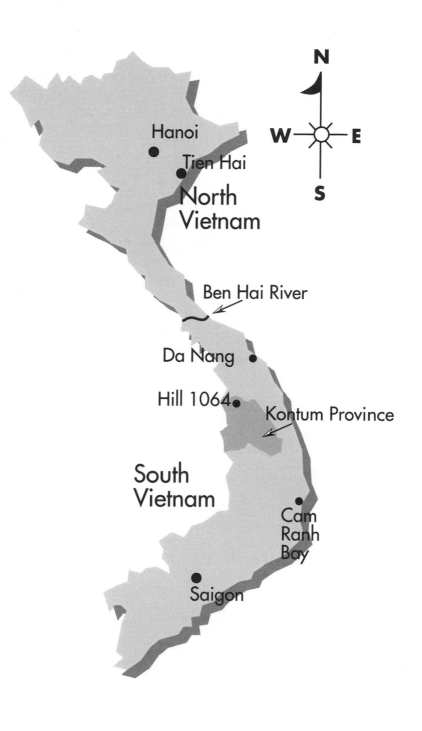

Do you want to experience the sights and sounds of this memorable story?

Kontum Diary "The Video" is now available only through this special mail offer! This award winning documentary of Paul Reed's journey back to Viet Nam is an excellent companion to the book. Follow Paul as he meets the North Vietnamese officer Nguyen van Nghia, who Paul

believed had died over two decades earlier in combat with his unit at Kontum. See and feel the emotion of these former, once hostile enemies as they reconcile at their wartime battlesite. View never before seen footage of North Vietnamese combat troops. Witness first hand how understanding can overcome hatred all because of a forgotten diary.

$19⁹⁵

"View the trip that changed my life."

PAUL REED

To order by credit card call:

1 (800) 806-4415

or send $19.95 plus $3.95 S&H by check or money order to :

CUSTOM VIDEO SERVICES
4505 Ratliff Lane
Dallas, TX 75248